D1085031

ARBITRARY BORDERS

Political Boundaries in World History

The Division of the Middle East
The Treaty of Sèvres

Northern Ireland and England
The Troubles

The Great Wall of China

The Green Line
The Division of Palestine

The Iron Curtain
The Cold War in Europe

The Mason–Dixon Line

Vietnam: The 17th Parallel

**Korea: The 38th Parallel and
the Demilitarized Zone**

The U.S.–Mexico Border
The Treaty of Guadalupe Hidalgo

**The Czech Republic:
The Velvet Revolution**

Louisiana Territory

**South Africa:
A State of Apartheid**

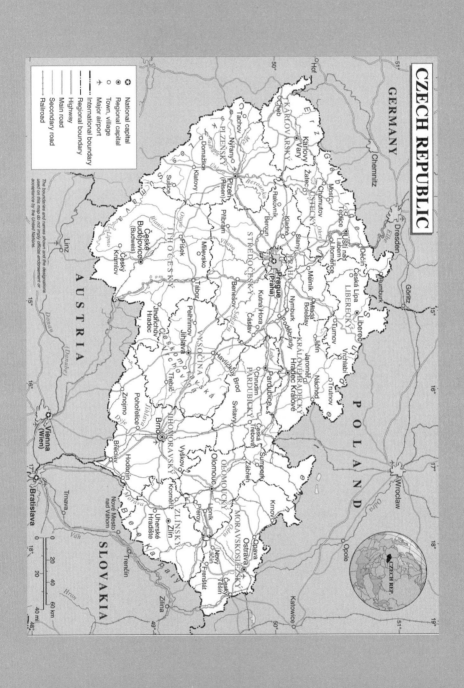

CZECH REPUBLIC

GERMANY

POLAND

AUSTRIA

SLOVAKIA

⊛	National capital
⊙	Regional capital
○	Town, village
✈	Major airport
–·–·–	International boundary
–––––	Regional boundary
–––––	Highway
–––––	Main road
–––––	Secondary road
┼┼┼┼	Railroad

The boundaries and names shown and the designations
used on this map do not imply official endorsement or
acceptance by the United Nations.

0 20 40 60 km
0 20 40 mi

CZECH REP.

Chemnitz
Dresden
Görlitz
Wrocław
Opole
Katowice

Linz
Vienna (Wien)
Bratislava
Trnava
Trenčín
Žilina

Cheb
Tachov
Karlovy Vary
KARLOVARSKÝ
Chomutov
Most
Teplice
Ústí nad Labem
Děčín
Rumburk
Šumperk
Česká Lípa
Liberec
LIBERECKÝ
Jablonec
Turnov
Jičín
Trutnov
Náchod
Jaroměř
KRÁLOVÉHRADECKÝ
Hradec Králové
Vrchlabí

Nýřany
Plzeň (Pilsen)
PLZEŇSKÝ
Klatovy
Domažlice
Sušice
Žatec
Rakovník
Beroun
Kladno
Slaný
ÚSTECKÝ
Litoměřice
Louny
Mělník
Nymburk
Poděbrady
Mladá Boleslav

Prague (Praha)
STŘEDOČESKÝ
Příbram
Benešov
Kutná Hora
Čáslav
Písek
Milevsko
Tábor

České Budějovice (Budweis)
Český Krumlov
JIHOČESKÝ
Jindřichův Hradec
Pelhřimov
Jihlava
VYSOČINA
Havlíčkův Brod
Třebíč
Znojmo
Pohořelice

PARDUBICKÝ
Pardubice
Chrudim
Svitavy
Česká Třebová
Ústí nad Orlicí
Zábřeh
OLOMOUCKÝ
Olomouc
Prostějov
Přerov
Hranice
Nový Jičín
Ostrava
Opava
Krnov
MORAVSKOSLEZSKÝ
Český Těšín
Frenštát
Frýdek-Místek

Brno
JIHOMORAVSKÝ
Břeclav
Hodonín
Vyškov
Kroměříž
Zlín
ZLÍNSKÝ
Uherské Hradiště
Nové Mesto nad Váhom

Ohře
Elbe
Berounka
Otava
Vltava
Blanice
Lužnice
Malše
Dyje
Jihlava
Morava
Sázava
Svratka
Labe

The Czech Republic: The Velvet Revolution

Robert C. Cottrell

Foreword by
Senator George J. Mitchell

Introduction by
James I. Matray
California State University, Chico

CHELSEA HOUSE
P U B L I S H E R S
A Haights Cross Communications Company

Philadelphia

FRONTIS A United Nations map of the Czech Republic, 2004.

CHELSEA HOUSE PUBLISHERS

VP, NEW PRODUCT DEVELOPMENT Sally Cheney
DIRECTOR OF PRODUCTION Kim Shinners
CREATIVE MANAGER Takeshi Takahashi
MANUFACTURING MANAGER Diann Grasse

Staff for THE CZECH REPUBLIC: THE VELVET REVOLUTION

EXECUTIVE EDITOR Lee Marcott
ASSISTANT EDITOR Alexis Browsh
PRODUCTION EDITOR Noelle Nardone
PHOTO EDITOR Sarah Bloom
SERIES DESIGNER Takeshi Takahashi
COVER DESIGNER Keith Trego
LAYOUT EJB Publishing Services

A Haights Cross Communications ✦ Company

www.chelseahouse.com

First Printing

9 8 7 6 5 4 3 2 1

Library of Congress Cataloging-in-Publication Data

Cottrell, Robert C., 1950-
  The Czech Republic : The Velvet Revolution / Robert C. Cottrell.
    p. cm. — (Arbitrary borders)
  Includes bibliographical references and index.
  ISBN 0-7910-8255-5 (hardcover)
  1. Czech Republic—History. I. Title: Velvet Revolution. II. Title. III. Series.
  DB2063.C68 2005
  943.71'03—dc22
                              2004025074

To Jeremy Kreisler

Contents

Foreword

Senator **George J. Mitchell**

I spent years working for peace in Northern Ireland and in the Middle East. I also made many visits to the Balkans during the long and violent conflict there.

Each of the three areas is unique; so is each conflict. But there are also some similarities: in each, there are differences over religion, national identity, and territory.

Deep religious differences that lead to murderous hostility are common in human history. Competing aspirations involving national identity are more recent occurrences, but often have been just as deadly.

Territorial disputes—two or more people claiming the same land—are as old as humankind. Almost without exception, such disputes have been a factor in recent conflicts. It is impossible to calculate the extent to which the demand for land—as opposed to religion, national identity, or other factors—figures in the motivation of people caught up in conflict. In my experience it is a substantial factor that has played a role in each of the three conflicts mentioned above.

In Northern Ireland and the Middle East, the location of the border was a major factor in igniting and sustaining the conflict. And it is memorialized in a dramatic and visible way: through the construction of large walls whose purpose is to physically separate the two communities.

In Belfast, the capital and largest city in Northern Ireland, the so-called "Peace Line" cuts through the heart of the city, right across urban streets. Up to thirty feet high in places, topped with barbed wire in others, it is an ugly reminder of the duration and intensity of the conflict.

In the Middle East, as I write these words, the government of Israel has embarked on a huge and controversial effort to construct a security fence roughly along the line that separates Israel from the West Bank.

Having served a tour of duty with the U.S. Army in Berlin, which was once the site of the best known of modern walls, I am skeptical of their long-term value, although they often serve short-term needs. But it cannot be said that such structures represent a new idea. Ancient China built the Great Wall to deter nomadic Mongol tribes from attacking its population.

In much the same way, other early societies established boundaries and fortified them militarily to achieve the goal of self-protection. Borders always have separated people. Indeed, that is their purpose.

This series of books examines the important and timely issue of the significance of arbitrary borders in history. Each volume focuses attention on a territorial division, but the analytical approach is more comprehensive. These studies describe arbitrary borders as places where people interact differently from the way they would if the boundary did not exist. This pattern is especially pronounced where there is no geographic reason for the boundary and no history recognizing its legitimacy. Even though many borders have been defined without legal precision, governments frequently have provided vigorous monitoring and military defense for them.

This series will show how the migration of people and exchange of goods almost always work to undermine the separation that borders seek to maintain. The continuing evolution of a European community provides a contemporary example illustrating this point, most obviously with the adoption of a single currency. Moreover, even former Soviet bloc nations have eliminated barriers to economic and political integration.

Globalization has emerged as one of the most powerful forces in international affairs during the twenty-first century. Not only have markets for the exchange of goods and services become genuinely worldwide, but instant communication and sharing of information have shattered old barriers separating people. Some scholars even argue that globalization has made the entire concept of a territorial nation-state irrelevant. Although the assertion is certainly premature and probably wrong, it highlights the importance of recognizing how borders often have reflected and affirmed the cultural, ethnic, or linguistic perimeters that define a people or a country.

Since the Cold War ended, competition over resources or a variety of interests threaten boundaries more than ever, resulting in contentious interaction, conflict, adaptation, and intermixture. How people define their borders is also a factor in determining how events develop in the surrounding region. This series will provide detailed descriptions of selected arbitrary borders in history with the objective of providing insights on how artificial boundaries separating people will influence international affairs during the next century.

Senator George J. Mitchell
October 2003

Introduction

James I. Matray
California State University, Chico

Throughout history, borders have separated people. Scholars have devoted considerable attention to assessing the significance and impact of territorial boundaries on the course of human history, explaining how they often have been sources of controversy and conflict. In the modern age, the rise of nation-states in Europe created the need for governments to negotiate treaties to confirm boundary lines that periodically changed as a consequence of wars and revolutions. European expansion in the nineteenth century imposed new borders on Africa and Asia. Many native peoples viewed these boundaries as arbitrary and, after independence, continued to contest their legitimacy. At the end of both world wars in the twentieth century, world leaders drew artificial and impermanent lines separating assorted people around the globe. Borders certainly are among the most important factors that have influenced the development of world affairs.

Chelsea House Publishers decided to publish a collection of books looking at arbitrary borders in history in response to the revival of the nuclear crisis in North Korea in October 2002. Recent tensions on the Korean peninsula are a direct consequence of Korea's partition at the 38th parallel at the end of World War II. Other nations in human history have suffered because of similar artificial divisions that have been the result of either international or domestic factors and often a combination of both. In the case of Korea, the United States and the Soviet Union decided in August 1945 to divide the country into two zones of military occupation ostensibly to facilitate the surrender of Japanese forces. However, a political contest was then underway inside Korea to determine the future of the nation after forty years of Japanese colonial rule. The Cold War then created two Koreas with sharply contrasting political, social, and economic systems that symbolized an ideological split among the Korean people. Borders separate people, but rarely prevent their economic, political, social, and cultural interaction. But in Korea, an artificial border has existed since 1945 as a nearly impenetrable barrier precluding meaningful contact between two portions of the same population. Ultimately, two authentic Koreas emerged, exposing how an arbitrary boundary can create circumstances resulting even in the permanent division of a homogeneous people in a historically united land.

Korea's experience in dealing with artificial division may well be unique, but it is not without historical parallels. The first set of books in this series on arbitrary boundaries will provide description and analysis of the division of the Middle East after World War I, the Iron Curtain in Central Europe during the Cold War, the United States-Mexico border, the 17th parallel in Vietnam, and the Mason-Dixon Line. A second set of books will address the Great Wall in China, the Green Line in Israel, and the 38th parallel and demilitarized zone in Korea. Finally, there will be volumes describing how discord over artificial borders in the Louisiana Territory, Northern Ireland, and Czechoslovakia reflected fundamental disputes about sovereignty, religion, and ethnicity. Admittedly, there are many significant differences between these boundaries, but these books will strive to cover as many common themes as possible. In so doing, each will help readers conceptualize how complex factors such as colonialism, culture, and economics determine the nature of contact between people along these borders. Although globalization has emerged as a powerful force working against the creation and maintenance of lines separating people, boundaries likely will endure as factors having a persistent influence on world events. This series of books will provide insights about the impact of arbitrary borders on human history and how such borders continue to shape the modern world.

James I. Matray
Chico, California
April 2004

1

The Munich Agreement

Distinguished political leaders responded quite differently following the announcement on September 30, 1938, of the Munich Agreement, which seemingly resolved disputes between Czechoslovakia and Germany over the Sudeten territory—an area in the Sudety mountains, whose 3.5 million residents boasted German roots. Reportedly suffering from ethnic discrimination, these German Czechs had supposedly clamored to be reunited with their ancestral land, a move that would require the redrawing of arbitrary territorial borders. At the time, Edouard Daladier, president of France, offered that the recently concluded conference—during which he negotiated with Germany's Adolf Hitler, Great Britain's Neville Chamberlain, and Italy's Benito Mussolini—had averted war and ensured "an honourable peace … for all nations."[1] Chamberlain, arriving at No. 10 Downing Street, his residence as British prime minister, waxed eloquently: "My good friends, this is the second time in our history that there has come back from Germany to Downing Street peace with honor." Chamberlain continued, "I believe it is peace for our time."[2]

Not all, however, were as pleased with the Munich Pact, as the agreement came to be called. Even before it was signed, Leon Blum, the former French head of state, indicated that the negotiations had probably averted war, but he felt "no joy and … find myself divided between a coward's relief and shame."[3] Speaking to the House of Commons, former British cabinet member Winston Churchill delivered a prescient speech on October 4, though it was hardly well-received:

> All is over. Silent, mournful, abandoned, broken Czechoslovakia recedes into the darkness…. [W]e have sustained a defeat without a war…. [W]e have passed an awful milestone in our history, when the whole equilibrium of Europe has been deranged, and that the terrible words have for [the] time being been pronounced against the Western Democracies: "Thou are weighed in the balance and found

wanting."... This is only the first sip, the first foretaste of a bitter cup....[4]

Czech leaders, who had not been allowed to directly participate in the negotiations that led to the loss of a great expanse of their nation's territory, also weighed in with their perspectives. Speaking for the government of Czech president Eduard Benes, Premier Jan Syrovy acknowledged, "If we must choose between the diminution of our territories and the death of our whole nation, it is our sacred duty to preserve the lives of our people, in order that ... we may not be obliged to abandon our belief that our nation will rise again, as it has done so often in the past." Chief of Staff Ludvik Krejci ordered his men to demonstrate "unconditional obedience" to the civilian leadership, claiming, "Our Army was not defeated. It has preserved unblemished its good repute....The Republic will have need of us."[5]

Notwithstanding such hopeful words, the Munich Pact foreshadowed the collapse of Czechoslovakia, which would occur within a matter of months. The agreement itself promised to establish new arbitrary borders for the still fledgling nation, birthed in the ashes of the Austro-Hungarian monarchy at the end of World War I. Coupled with additional provisions demanded only days following the declaration that an agreement had been reached, the pact resulted in German occupation of more than one-third of the western and eastern Czech provinces of Bohemia and Moravia, respectively, where some 800,000 Czechs dwelled. Additional encroachments were undertaken by Poland and Hungary. Altogether, Czechoslovakia relinquished nearly 16,000 square miles of its landscape, along with almost 5,000,000 of its 14,500,000 inhabitants. In November, the newly named Czecho-Slovakia was proclaimed a nation, with its autonomous states: Bohemia and Moravia, Slovakia, and Ruthenia.

Thus, well before the complete German takeover in early 1939, a greatly truncated Czech state emerged. This was the fate of the one democracy to emerge along the border of the Soviet

Union in the aftermath of the most horrific martial conflagration humankind had yet witnessed. The treatment afforded Czechoslovakia resulted from deliberate policies on the part of German leader Adolf Hitler, who recognized the Czechs as Slavs, a group he considered an inferior people, and because of the failure of the republic's erstwhile allies to come to its defense. In a meeting with other members of the Nazi Party in early 1933 shortly after taking power, Hitler discussed the need for *Lebensraum*, "conquest of new living space in the east and ruthless Germanization of the latter."[6]

As early as May 1935, German field marshal Werner von Blomberg—who headed the Wehrmacht, or the German armed forces—secretly ordered the devising of operational plans for a strike against Czechoslovakia. Significantly, as Gerhard L. Weinberg notes, there existed remarkable agreement among top German government officials "on the issue of making Czechoslovakia disappear from the map of Europe."[7] Following the signing of the Czechoslovak-Soviet Treaty of Mutual Assistance in 1935, Hitler viewed Czechoslovakia as "the spearhead of Soviet penetration into Central Europe," Telford Taylor indicates. As German remilitarization occurred, von Blomberg issued on June 24, 1937, the secret memorandum entitled "Directive 1937/38," which discussed "Probable War Contingencies," including Operation Green. That plan foresaw "a surprise German operation against Czechoslovakia in order to parry the imminent attack of a superior enemy coalition."[8]

The next important move involved the so-called Hossbach protocol of November 5, 1937, drafted by a German colonel. That protocol resulted from a meeting involving top military and government leaders, including Blomberg, Hermann Goering, who guided Germany's rearmament program, and Hitler, in which the Führer referred to Czechoslovakia in discussing *Lebensraum*: "For the improvement of our politico-military position," he declared, "our first objective, in the event of being embroiled in war, must be to overthrow Czechoslovakia and Austria simultaneously in order to remove the threat to our flank." Already, Hitler believed, the English and the French had apparently "tacitly written off the Czechs." When war arrived, he planned to "carry through the campaign against the Czechs ... with lightning speed."[9] For Hitler, control over Czechoslovakia would ensure German dominance in central Europe. German hegemony, in turn, required a takeover of the Sudetenland, which boasted a series of Czech fortifications intended to withstand a German assault. Additionally, the conquest of Czechoslovakia and Austria, Hitler reasoned, would allow for the garnering of food for millions of Germans if the forced emigration of two million Czechs and one million Austrians should occur.

Speaking before the German Reichstag on February 20, 1938, Hitler referred ominously to the "ten million unredeemed Germans in the adjacent States."[10] Then, on March 12, 1938, German soldiers swept into Austria, with Hitler proclaiming an *Anschluss* (union) with Germany; no Czech fortifications existed along the border with Austria. The following day, the socialist Leon Blum returned to power in France; his government indicated it would assist Czechoslovakia in the event that an attack was forthcoming. The English government, headed by Prime Minister Chamberlain, refused to deliver a comparable statement. Chamberlain did inform his cabinet that the prevention of "an occurrence of similar events in Czechoslovakia" was important.[11] President Benes of Czechoslovakia sought to obtain backing from Great Britain and France before dealing with Germany in a dignified and courageous manner. But the British government refused to deliver commitments that risked war, and instead urged the Czechs to devise "a direct settlement with the Sudetendeutsch."[12]

Encouraged by Hitler, Konrad Heinlein, who had earlier established the Sudeten German Party, delivered unreasonable demands, insisting on complete equality for Czechs and Germans within the Czech government, the termination of past injustices and the payment of reparations, and "full liberty to profess German nationality and German political philosophy."[13] To the British government, Heinlein posed possible resolutions to the conundrum, including "autonomy within the Czechoslovak state … plebiscite probably leading to the Anschluss … war." All the while, the Magyars (Hungarians), Slovak nationalists, and Poles in Teschen expressed discontent of their own.

The planning for Operation Green continued at the highest levels of the German regime, with Hitler stating in mid-May, "It is not my intention to crush Czechoslovakia militarily in the immediate future."[14] Nevertheless, the mobilization of Czech force, which prevented a rapid move against Czech fortifications in the Sudeten districts, angered him. On May 20, the new commander-in-chief of the German military, Wilhelm Keitel, offered a revised plan for Operation Green, envisioning the quashing of Czechoslovakia militarily, even if no pretext for invasion existed, along with the rapid-fire occupation of both Bohemia and Moravia. Ten days later, Hitler signed the directive, whose preamble indicated that

> It is my unalterable decision to smash Czechoslovakia by military action in the near future…. It is essential to create a situation within the first two or three days which demonstrates to enemy states which wish to intervene the hopelessness of the Czech military position, and also provides an incentive to those states which have territorial claims upon Czechoslovakia to join in immediately against her.

Operation Green called for Czechoslovakia to be subdued by October 1.[15]

By this point, the British government and a French administration, now headed by Edouard Daladier, were insisting that Prague resolve the minority problem involving Sudeten Germans. During the next two months, Czech government officials and representatives from the Sudeten German Party conducted futile discussions regarding the purported grievances of German Czechs. At the same time, demonstrations occurred calling for Slovak autonomy; those were spearheaded by Andrei Hlinka, who headed the right-wing Slovak Catholic Party. The German general staff completed its final planning for Operation

Green; on July 7, General Keitel informed Hitler, who considered the continued existence of Czechoslovakia to be "unbearable," that "there is no danger of a preventive war against Germany."[16] Should such an unlikely development unfold, Keitel continued, it would necessarily "begin with the destruction of Czechoslovakia." Nevertheless, the British government soon received word from a German envoy that Hitler desired "to see the Czech affair dealt with amicably."[17]

General Walter von Brauchitsch informed Hitler that top military officers feared Operation Green would culminate in another World War and ultimate disaster for Germany. Consequently, Hitler turned to a second rung of German military officers, urging them to support Operation Green. Speaking for three hours on August 10, Hitler insisted that the plan involved "the greatness of Germany … brothers in race … three million Germans oppressed by the Czechs."[18] Five days later, Hitler harangued his senior commanders, indicating that *Lebensraum* demanded action, while Czechoslovakia, which he termed the "Soviet Russian aircraft carrier," had to be destroyed.[19] The great European democracies, he predicted, would not intervene. On August 24, 1938, Colonel Alfred Jodl sent a note to Hitler, declaring that "Operation Green will be set off by an incident in Czechoslovakia that will provide Germany with an excuse for military intervention."[20] Three days later, General Ludwig Beck, Chief of Staff of the German army resigned, having failed to convince Hitler to discard the plan to invade Czechoslovakia.

Worrying that Benes was proving too accommodating, albeit reluctantly, members of the Sudeten German Party helped to trigger an incident on September 7 involving the supposed mistreatment of a party deputy during the midst of street action. Speaking in Nuremberg, Nazi leaders Goebbels and Goering reviled the Czech state. Goebbels termed the events in Czechoslovakia "particularly menacing," with Prague said to be "the organizing center of Bolshevik plots against Europe." Goering cried out, "We know how intolerable it is that that little fragment of a nation down there—goodness knows where it hails from—should persistently oppress and interfere with a highly civilized people. But we know that it is not these absurd pygmies who are responsible: Moscow and the eternal Jewish-Bolshevik rabble are behind it."[21]

The London *Times* suggested that the Czechs consider ceding the Sudetenland to Germany. On September 12, 1938, Hitler delivered a speech to Nazi Party members in Nuremberg bemoaning the supposed fate of Sudeten Germans, whose "wretchedness," he claimed, "is indescribable. The Czechs want to wipe them out."[22] With Hitler demanding self-determination for the Germans in Czechoslovakia, disorder broke out in the Sudetenland, resulting in the sending in of Czech troops and the departure of Heinlein from Czechoslovakia. All the while, plans for Operation Green remained in place.

To Hitler's surprise, British prime minister Chamberlain sought a face-to-face encounter. When they met in Berchtesgaden, Hitler—who remained committed to Czechoslovakia's destruction—exclaimed, "The thing has got to be settled at once ... and I am prepared to risk a world war rather than allow this to drag on." Regarding the Czech state, Hitler asserted, "If Sudeten Germans come into the Reich, then the Hungarian minority would secede, the Polish minority would secede, the Slovak minority would secede—and what was left would be so small that [Chamberlain] would not bother his head about it." Supposedly speaking only for himself, Chamberlain indicated that he "had nothing to say against the secession of the Sudeten Germans from the rest of Czechoslovakia."[23]

While Chamberlain sent back hopeful reports to his cabinet, Duff Cooper, First Lord of the Admiralty, indicated it was "difficult to believe that the self-determination of the Sudeten Germans was Hitler's last aim." As the Czech military occupied frontier areas, the French government sought Great Britain's agreement to "join in some form of international guarantee of Czechoslovakia," to help convince Benes to cede the Sudetenland.[24] By September 21, British and French representatives had pressured Czechoslovakia to accept a plan to have an

A weeping Sudeten woman salutes the triumphant Nazi German dictator Adolf Hitler in 1938, after the Sudetenland was ceded to Germany as part of the Munich Pact.

international body redraw its borders in return for Britain's promise that it would help to guarantee the new boundaries against an unprovoked attack.

Feeling "disgracefully betrayed," Czech prime minister Benes announced the agreement; this was followed by angry responses and demonstrations in Prague, along with condemnations of the Czech leader. Seeking to calm matters, Benes spoke on national radio, expressing confidence in the future: "I have never feared, and I do not fear for the future of our nation…. Have no fear for

Sudeten German refugees wait to board one of the trains at the Klingenthal station in Czechoslovakia in September 1938, as agreed to in the Munich Pact. The German-speaking Czechs were fleeing Sudetenland to a refugee camp in Germany.

the nation and the state. The nation has deep roots. Czechoslovakia will not perish."[25]

Notwithstanding Benes's decision to accept the Anglo-French proposal, Sudeten Germans grabbed hold of German-dominated towns as German divisions mobilized along the Czech border. On September 22, Chamberlain informed Hitler that the Sudetenland would be transferred to Germany, but Hitler insisted that German forces be allowed to immediately occupy the ceded territory. The next day, Hitler sent a lengthy letter to Chamberlain, indicating that "with best will ... I have proposed, as the future border, in the event of a peaceful settlement, that racial frontier which represents, I am sure, a just compromise between the two national groups and which also takes into account the existence of large linguistic enclaves."[26] Subsequently, Chamberlain received a memorandum from Hitler demanding, among other matters, the removal of all

Czech military and government forces from the Sudetenland, and the holding of a plebiscite in evacuated territories. Hitler promised that this involved "the last territorial demand which he had to make in Europe."[27]

The French and Czech governments rejected the ultimatums, with Czechoslovakia undertaking a general mobilization. Czech cabinet member Jan Masaryk informed Chamberlain, "The Czechoslovak nation will never consent to be an enslaved people!" Writing to Prague, he stated, "Chamberlain is really surprised that we should not be prepared to withdraw our troops from the fortified lines on our frontiers."[28] The French cabinet members agreed that "Herr Hitler's object was to destroy Czechoslovakia and to dominate Europe." Soon, both the English and French leaders determined that implementation of the German plan "would be to cut Czechoslovakia to pieces and leave her more completely at the mercy of Germany."[29] By September 26, the Hungarian Foreign Ministry warned that if Germany occupied the Sudetenland, then Hungary and Poland would also take over minority areas in Czechoslovakia.

Hitler and Chamberlain met yet again, along with Daladier and Mussolini, this time in Munich on September 29 and 30, 1938. They produced the Munich Agreement, calling for the delivery of the Sudetenland to Germany, with Czech evacuation to be completed by October 10, no strategic installations to be destroyed, and Czechoslovakia to be held accountable for ensuring that was so. An international commission would determine what additional area that Germany could occupy, the framework for plebiscites, where international forces would be stationed, and the location of the international boundaries, which were to be protected by Great Britain and France "against 'unprovoked aggression.'"[30] Both Chamberlain and Daladier returned home to cheering throngs.

Czechoslovakia was not represented at the conference that determined its fate and redrew its borders. The Munich Agreement ensured, as Alfred Jodl admitted, that "Czechoslovakia as a power is out."[31] It resulted in the turning over to Germany of 34 percent of Czechoslovakia's population, 29 percent of its landscape, and 40 percent of its industrial capacity, along with its fortifications. The agreement made still more precarious the continued existence of the small Central European democratic state, founded in the ashes of World War I and now torn apart as an international conflagration loomed ahead. The pact left Czechoslovakia, with its much-reduced borders arbitrarily drawn, almost wholly vulnerable to additional assaults on its territorial integrity, as would soon be demonstrated.

2

Early Czech History

Comprised of 78,864 square miles, the Czech Republic is located in the center of Europe, bordered by Germany, Austria, Poland, and Slovakia. It contains Bohemia in the west and Moravia in the east. While Moravia's northern sectors once belonged to Silesia, the present Czech Republic possesses the borders it did 1,000 years ago.

Ringed by mountain chains, Bohemia exists on a 500-meter plateau, with the Vltava and Labe rivers forming a basin. The Bohemian or Sumava Forest, the Krusne hory or Ore Mountains, and the Krkonose or Giant Mountains provide territorial borders alongside neighboring states. Hilly Moravia features the Moravian Gate, frequently used as a route of invasion. The Little and White Carpathian Mountains—Male and Bile Karpaty—offer a buttress against Slovakia to the East.

Beginning around the seventh century B.C., Iron-Age settlements founded by prehistoric peoples began appearing in both Bohemia and Moravia. Eventually, Celtic tribes, known by the Romans as the *Boii*, resided in the land called *Boiohemum*, employing furnaces to smelt metal, tools, jewelry, and beads, and engaging in various trading patterns with other peoples. Around 500 B.C., Germanic forces, including the Marcomans and the Kvades, moved into Bohemia and Moravia respectively. In the first century A.D., efforts were undertaken to establish statelike apparatuses in both Bohemia and Moravia. Confrontations with Roman legions occurred, while the Battle of Nations at Chalons-sur-Marne led to the vanquishing of both the Marcomans and the Kvades.

Over the span of several centuries, Slavic tribesmen such as the Czechs came to the region, eventually driving westward around 500 A.D. as the Frankish empire was emerging. Nomadic Asiatic Avars took control for a period, but the Slavs reasserted themselves in 623 or 624, led by Samo, a Frankish trader who temporarily united Bohemia, Moravia, Lusatia, eastern Bavaria, and sections of Slovakia and Hungary into a tenuous merchant empire. Following his death in 658, this trading network collapsed.

By the ninth century, the Greater Moravian Empire material-
ized, with Moravia and sections of Slovakia serving as its center.
The empire's rulers incorporated Christianity from the
Byzantine Empire in an attempt to ward off assaults by the
Franks; nevertheless, the influence of the Western Church
proved considerable. In the last part of the ninth century, a pair
of missionaries, the saints Cyril and Methodius, helped to craft
the first Slavic alphabet. Notwithstanding religious and linguistic transformations, Greater Moravia, which had come to
include Czechs and Slovaks, disintegrated in the midst of an
invasion by the Magyars, or Hungarians. As the empire crumbled, Bohemia emerged, to be led by the Premyslid dynasty for
four centuries. The famed and later sainted tribal chief, Prince
Vaclav, guided Bohemia from about 924–935, seeking amicable
relations with the Franks and displaying Christian fervor. By the
close of the tenth century, the Premyslid dominance included
Moravia.

During this same period, Bohemia became part of the Holy
Roman Empire. A century or so later, Bohemia included sections
of Austria and Poland. As was true throughout Europe, power
struggles continued to play out between Bohemia's kings and its
aristocracy.

Over the course of the twelfth and thirteenth centuries,
German immigrants moved into mining territory near the Czech
frontier and to towns across Bohemia in particular. During the
early thirteenth century, the Czech kingdom proved instrumental in preventing Central Europe from being overrun by Tartars
when Vaclav I bested them in Moravia. The Luxemburg dynasty
began in the early fourteenth century, with three kings of
Bohemia also heading the Holy Roman Empire. Bohemia's ascen-
dancy peaked during the tenure of Emperor Charles IV (reign
1348–1378), who founded Prague University, the first such institution in Central Europe, in 1348, and helped to turn Prague,
already a thriving commercial center, into the most important
city in the empire. Charles IV became known as both "Father of
the Country" and "the most European of emperors."[32]

The Holy Roman Emperor Charles IV (1348–1378) with his hands folded in prayer, a detail from a votive panel by a Czech master. Charles IV became known as the "Father of the Country" for his work to make Prague a thriving intellectual and commercial center throughout the Czech kingdom and Europe.

Prague also became the focal point of exciting ideas coursing through Europe by the close of the fourteenth century. This resulted in the recasting of arbitrary borders of a religious nature. A campaign to reform the Roman Catholic Church occurred in Bohemia during the latter years of Charles IV and throughout the reign of Vaclav IV (1378–1419). Political conflicts also developed between Czechs and Germans, with the former demanding improved representation in various towns, including Prague. Also increasingly in vogue were the ideas of the English religious reformer John Wycliffe, who denounced the Church's wealth, power, and papal dominance, and insisted that ordinary people should be exposed to religious texts. While Wycliffe was condemned as a heretic, his tenets appealed to many students and teachers, including Jan Hus, a theologian and rector of Charles University.

For his part, Hus criticized such Church practices as the selling of indulgences and the Inquistion while calling for services to be delivered in the Czech language, all of which led him to be branded a heretic. Excommunicated by the Church, Hus, who insisted that "Truth prevails," was burned at the stake in 1415. Within four years, the religiously inspired, class-oriented, nationalistic Hussites Wars broke out, pitting followers of Hus, the martyred national hero, and King Vaclav IV, against supporters of the pope. The Hussites included the radical Taborites, who favored an egalitarian society; wealthy burghers from Prague; and Protestant nobles, with the latter two groups both fearing the Taborites.

Once the Catholic armies were defeated, the Protestant and Catholic lords united to overcome the Taborites at Lipany in 1436. Rome was compelled to accept something of a Czech reformed church, while the ideal of "non-violence and non-resistance to evil," A.H. Hermann records, was held aloft by Petr Chelcicky, an itinerant Bohemian preacher who provided the foundation for the Czech Brethren.[33] To placate the papacy and prevent imperial intervention, King Jiri of Podebrad felt compelled to repress the Czech Brethren, a development that hardly encouraged a sense of nationalism.

Polish kings had served as titular rulers of Bohemia, although real power resided with Czech nobles. Following the defeat of a Czech army and the murder of a Czech king by Turks in 1526, the nobles accepted Ferdinand I of Habsburg as their king. Ferdinand relocated various government offices to Vienna and centralized administration, thus diminishing the role performed by national parliaments. Czech nobles continued to hold large estates and to select their own rulers, while the Protestant Reformation, influenced by Martin Luther and John Calvin, made additional inroads among the general populace. Recurrent assaults by Turkish forces only strengthened the hand of the Catholic Habsburgs, who awarded large grants of territory to those residing in other lands.

Believing that the Habsburgs had failed to ensure religious tolerance, Czech nobles revolted in 1618, naming a Protestant king of Bohemia. The conflict became the religiously-waged Thirty Years' War, which essentially pitted militant Calvinists against ardent Catholics. In 1620, the Habsburgs prevailed at the Battle of White Mountain, resulting in their determination to quash Czech Protestantism and nationalism altogether; thus, the Habsburgs felt compelled to reaffirm religiously drawn arbitrary borders.

Charges of high treason were leveled at 26 Protestant leaders along with a single Catholic ally, all of whom were mutilated and beheaded at the Old Town Square in the center of Prague. The Habsburgs confiscated the property of Czech nobles, forcibly converted peasants to Catholicism, and compelled other Protestants to choose between conversion or emigration; those who remained were also subjected to a process of Germanization. As many as 300,000 individuals, including the enlightened Czech Brethren pastor Jan Amos Komensky, known as Comenius, chose to depart, as did many intellectuals and peasants alike.

Bohemia split into the provinces of Bohemia, Moravia, and Silesia, all headed by representatives of the Habsburgs, who made themselves into a hereditary dynasty. A new constitution, the Renewed Establishment, allowed for Roman Catholicism only. Czech independence and some 40 percent of Czech territory had been lost by the time the Peace of Westphalia was

Bohemian religious reformer Jan Hus (1372–1415) being burned at the stake for heresy, on July 6, 1415. Hus's crimes included criticizing such Church practices as the selling of indulgences and the Inquisition, as well as not saying Mass in the language of the people. His death sparked off the religious Hussite wars, which lasted about 15 years.

drafted, ending the Thirty Years' War; no Czech representatives had been welcomed at the peace conference.

For nearly 300 years the Czechs would be subjects of the Austrian Empire, with the Czech language surviving only in Slovakia. The Counter-Reformation, exemplified by Jesuit censors burning books, took hold during the seventeenth century. As aristocrats and the bourgeoisie deferred to the Habsburgs, only the peasants remained willing to contest difficult times, responding with a series of unsuccessful revolts in both the seventeenth and eighteenth centuries.

The Habsburgs suffered a setback of their own in 1741, when Frederick II of Prussia took control of Silesia, then the most economically developed Czech land. To the dismay of Maria Theresa, who succeeded her father, Charles VI, Britain had urged her to cede Silesia to Frederick. Prussia also appeared primed to strike at both Bohemia and Moravia. Maria Theresa refused to give way easily, conducting three wars in an attempt to regain Silesia. In 1742, Prague was held by Bavarian and French forces, who also temporarily took control of Bohemia. Maria Theresa attained peace by signing the treaty of Breslau, which allowed her to reacquire Prague and Frederick to retain Silesia, thereby reshaping the region's arbitrary borders.

Ultimately, Maria Theresa was able to hold on to only Bohemia and Moravia, although Klasko, a Bohemian province, was lost. At the same time, she became archduchess of Austria as well as queen of both Hungary and Bohemia, and largely controlled state affairs following the appointment in 1745 of her husband, Francis I, as the Holy Roman Emperor. Maria Theresa discarded the Czech Court Office, stabling the central administrative and financial departments that ruled over Czech and Austrian Habsburg territories. The Czech kingdom appeared to further dissipate as Czech nobles lost more power and Habsburg emperors stopped being referred to as Czech kings. On a more positive note, with customs tariffs discarded and Czech textiles and glassworks in demand, Czech mining, trade, and industry were revitalized by the end of the eighteenth century. Under Joseph II, who became the Holy Roman Emperor in 1765, serfdom disappeared from Czech crown lands in 1781, allowing surplus agricultural workers to obtain employment in industry.

That same year, Joseph II issued the Toleration Patent, which seemingly discarded arbitrary borders of a religious nature. Most significantly, this helped to open frontier lands to Protestant influences during a period when capitalist developments were already weakening feudal ties. Jews too appeared to be liberated, at least to a certain extent, after centuries of oppression.

From the twelfth century onward, Jews could be found throughout Bohemia and Moravia, and had settled in Prague even earlier. Forced to dwell in ghettoes, they were tied to the Crown, which extorted taxes from them but failed to prevent repeated pogroms; indeed, during troublesome times, the monarchy often made Jews scapegoats. For a brief period during the thirteenth century, Jews, some of whom were involved in important commercial ventures, were deemed to possess equality before the law, but such protection vanished when trading patterns withered.

Joseph II now hoped that Jewish merchants and craftsmen would help to energize the Czech economy. Under both Maria Theresa and Joseph II, Jews also took advantage of expanded educational opportunities, benefiting from secular schooling that emphasized basic literacy.

As A.H. Hermann notes, at the time of Joseph II's death in 1790, those who dwelled on Czech soil "formed two nations." The first, which was Czech-speaking, included peasants and inhabitants of small towns. The second, German-speaking, featured nobles and wealthier merchants. Hermann suggests that only the latter group "counted as the political nation, which was still geographically conceived." Class and economic barriers remained more pronounced than linguistic ones. However, change was in the offing, spurred by Joseph II's abolition of serfdom and various educational and legal transformations.

The pace of those changes was only accelerated by the wars in Europe that swirled around the French Revolution and, by the last half of the 1790s, the antics of Napoleon Bonaparte. The "ideology of national liberation" swept across the European continent, while martial affairs altered economic circumstances.[34] Inflationary pressures actually benefited peasants, who could pay taxes more easily at the same time their foodstuffs became more valuable. In addition, the continental economic blockade by Napoleon encouraged the growth of the Czech textile, sugar, and iron and steel production industries. Improved economic circumstances, in turn, allowed for population increases in Bohemia, Moravia, and parts of Silesia.

All the while, the seeds of cultural nationalism were being

planted, ironically enough with considerable Germanic influence, pointing to the artificiality of arbitrary borders associated
with statecraft. Bernard Bolzano, the Catholic philosopher,
mathematician, and theologian, wrote in German but greatly
impressed Czech intellectuals. His "On Love for the Homeland"
asked, "What land should each individual consider as his homeland, and how far should its borders extend?" Answering his own
query, Bolzano declared that "The land, in which you live, is your
true homeland," and indicated that "[the homeland] extends as
far as the state extends of whom we are the subjects by law."
Bolzano continued, "Ordinarily, the borders of the homeland do
not coincide with an individual land and nation," and he sought
to convince his students to "love and embrace one another as
children of a single shared homeland!"

Other authors, including Gelasius Dobner, who was later
called "the first and mighty awakener of the Czech nation," and
Joseph Dobrovsky, who in 1792 wrote the *History of Czech
Language and Literature*, also helped to revitalize Czech culture.
Josef Jungmann, through his *History of Czech Literature or
Systematic Survey of Czech Writings, with a Short History of the
Nation, Education and Language*, which first appeared in 1825,
attempted to rescue the Czech language, as did his *Czech-
German Dictionary* (1834–39). The leading Czech historian of
the nineteenth century, Frantisek Palacky, who sought to culti-
vate a national consciousness, produced *The History of the Czech
Nation in Bohemia and Moravia*, the first volume of which came
out in German in 1836. He came to be known as the "Father of
the Nation."[35]

The heightening of Czech nationalism among intellectuals
helped to produce, as Derek Sayer writes, "a vocabulary of
national identity."[36]So too did growing frustration with the
seemingly absolute power held by the Habsburg state, which had
resulted in a nearly impotent Bohemian Diet (assembly) and
heavy-handed practices by the Police and Censorship Court
Bureau, run by Count J. Sedlnitzky. These developments made
Czechs receptive to the revolutionary tide that swept across

Europe in 1848, beginning with the ouster of the Orleanist monarchy in Paris and carrying over to many Central European states.

Inequities heightened by the industrial revolution and frustration with autocratic practices helped to spur the wave of revolts that threatened to topple other regimes. In Central Europe, the Habsburg emperor dismissed foreign minister Klemens Metternich and selected a new government, promising constitutional governance. Palacky, who supported Austro-Slavism but opposed pan-Germanism, turned down a request that Czechs be represented in an Imperial Diet in Frankfurt. Nevertheless, in April, Czechs were offered their own Constitutional Assembly, easier access to the franchise (the vote), the reestablishment of royal offices in Prague, and acknowledgment that the Czech language had equal status with German.

Nationalist and socialist forces, however, were disturbed by the subsequent appointment of Prince Windischgraetz to head the Prague garrison. A series of clashes occurred between soldiers on one side and students and workers on the other. In May, Windischgraetz stationed his troops on Prague's outskirts.

On June 2, the Slavic Congress met in Prague, with, as Stanley Z. Pech suggests, "an intoxicating atmosphere of 'Slavic nationalism'" clearly present. Radicals soon gained the upper hand over figures like Palacky, who considered the empire to be necessary to safeguard Czech national security. The Congress proclaimed a Manifesto to European Nations that praised "the Slavs, with whom liberty has from time immemorial been loved the more devoutly, the less they manifested a lust for domination and subjugation," in contrast to the "Romance and Germanic nations."[37]

As the Congress continued to meet, students and factory workers gathered in the center of Prague, but military forces soon attacked them. With radicals advancing to the barricades, Prince Windischgraetz pulled his troops back from the city only to conduct an artillery bombardment, which blunted the revolt; Windischgraetz established a military dictatorship. Intellectuals, the middle class, and peasants all stood apart from the fighting, which involved no more than 1,500 students, workers, and other individuals. The Czech bourgeoisie, aligned with Bohemian and Moravian nobles, desired a return to the aristocratically drawn constitution of the Czech monarchy under Habsburg rule.

Thus, lacking sufficient support, the Czech uprising, like the other revolutions that unfolded in 1848 and 1849, quickly dissipated. Nevertheless, change was forthcoming, with the new emperor, Franz Josef I, emancipating the peasants and undertaking the industrialization of Bohemia and Moravia. Mining for iron ore and coking coal intensified; the Trade Act of 1859 fostered capitalistic economic development, which inevitably furthered arbitrary borders based on class; and imperial officials removed tariff barriers that affected Czech industry.

Still, Czechs considered themselves tied to a movement that would soon transform the European continent. The failed revolutions of 1848 and 1849 imparted a legacy: the flourishing of nationalism in the period ahead, which resulted in the establishment of modern national states, whose territorial boundaries were necessarily arbitrarily devised. The creation of an independent Czechoslovakian nation, with its own clearly defined borders, would have to await several decades more, but the failed revolution of 1848, coupled with the cultural nationalism that had recently been fostered, provided seeds for that development. Those seeds were yet to sprout, but when they did, nationalists would call on Czech history, including periods characterized by territorial integrity as well as those in which religious, political, and cultural figures insisted on Czech autonomy. At the same time, they would be saddled with a past sprinkled with shifting artificial boundaries of a geographic and religious cast.

3

A Nationalist
Revival

Although the Austrian monarchy supported economic transformation in the empire, it strove to maintain arbitrary borders of a political or ideological stripe, suspending the constitution of 1849. Prime Minister Alexander Bach reached an agreement with the papacy that restored privileges Joseph II had removed from the church, such as stewardship of early education. Bach also attempted to curb nationalistic sentiments arising in places like Bohemia and Moravia, reasoning that imperial control would be heightened if German became the universal language of the emperor's subjects. Increasingly, Czechs were compelled to turn to Vienna, the capital of the empire, to resolve disputes with Germans.

Nationalist leaders like Frantisek Palacky, Frantisek Ladislav Rieger, and Karel Havlicek opted for retirement, expatriation, or continued battles with authority figures as repression took hold, resulting in the shutting down of Czech nationalist newspapers and the holding of trials designed to gag imperial critics. As the 1850s unfolded, no free Czech press still existed; authorities silenced the Brothers of the Red Banner, a student republican organization; and police surveillance mounted in intensity in an effort to strengthen ideologically focused arbitrary borders. A new generation of cultural nationalists, including Bozena Nemcova and Jan Neruda, attempted to keep Czech identity alive. Their efforts, and those of other Czech patriots, would help to retrigger national pride, as Josef Kalvoda records in his *Genesis of Czechoslovakia* (1986).

The makeup of the empire changed following the defeat of Austrian forces by both France and the Italian kingdom of Piedmont at Magenta and Solferino in 1859, which led to the discarding of the Bach system and the unification of Italian citystates. These developments, in turn, helped to bring about a Czech political revival, for the Habsburg's near absolutism had been called into question and a new wave of nationalism was taking effect. Rieger established a new newspaper, *The National Gazette*, which urged autonomy for Bohemia, Moravia, and

Silesia. Czech aristocrats proved sympathetic, resulting in the formation of the Old Czech Party.

However, Czech nationalists were hardly pleased that imperial reforms, which led to the reestablishment of local diets, or parliaments, ensured that Czechs were unequally represented there or in the Imperial Diet. Figures like Palacky and Rieger were uncertain whether they should even refuse to be seated in Vienna. Another group of nationalists, later referred to as the Young Czechs, including Karel Sladkovsky and Prince Rudolf Thurn-Taxis, wanted to adopt a tougher stance against imperial dominance and mold a more liberal party. Nationalistic sentiments in Czech lands became more decidedly anti-German rather than supporting the older notion of an independent Czech state made up of Czech- and German-speaking residents. Consequently, many Czech nobles with German origins became increasingly alienated from Czech politics, ensuring that the Czech cause possessed less weight in Vienna. At the same time, this development ultimately allowed Czech society to incorporate more liberal and democratic ideals.

By 1865, all Czech representatives had abstained from serving in the Imperial Diet. In a series of articles, Palacky insisted that Czechs would accept only a federal government, not one that was centralist—which would enable Germans to hold sway over both Magyars and Slavs—nor one that was dualist, which would necessarily be anti-Slavic. Obviously cognizant of Czechs' autonomous past and demand for recognition, the great historian appreciated that "they would settle for nothing short of equality in the Empire or for its destruction."[38]

In 1866, the German kingdom of Prussia defeated Austria at Hradec Kralove, located in northern Bohemia, during the Seven Weeks' War. This compelled Austria to grant sweeping concessions to Hungary, which led, in December 1867, to the splitting of the Habsburg Empire into Austria and Hungary. Thus, the Habsburg Empire itself experienced wholesale transformation with these new, broadly determined artificial boundaries, even though the two states still possessed a common army, central

finances, foreign policy, and allegiance to Franz Josef, who supported the promulgation of a new constitution that drew considerable opposition from Bohemia and Moravia.

During the fighting, Prussian leaders had indicated they
would support Czech independence, but even the younger
Czech nationalists refused to support a break with the Austrian
empire. Thus, the Czechs had achieved little as the war ended,
in contrast to the Magyars, who had posed such a threat to
Austrian rule. The Czechs refused to attend the Bohemian and
Moravian Diets, and Palacky and Rieger attempted to garner
support from both France's Napoleon III and Russia's
Alexander II. Large demonstrations occurred in Czech territory
calling for a reduction in land taxes, improved working conditions, and an end to social discrimination. Nationalist sentiment
rose, with many insisting on Czech-controlled assemblies in
Bohemia and Moravia.

The Austrian regime declared martial law in Prague in 1868,
incarcerating hundreds of political prisoners, forbidding various public demonstrations, and breaking up others. Still, the
protest continued, gaining in strength, while Rieger again
sought backing from Napoleon III. Austria became more concerned following the Franco-Prussian War of 1870–1871, which
enabled Prussia to stand as the center of a new German empire,
led by Chancellor Otto Bismarck. Suddenly more determined to
placate the Czechs, Franz Josef, who had been crowned Czech
king, agreed to the Fundamental Articles in 1871, which called
for granting Bohemia more autonomy in taxation, policing
powers, and education. Opposition by the Hungarians and
Germans residing in Bohemia led to the quashing of the proposals, however. Moravia, in contrast, was to receive no such
favored treatment.

In 1874, the Young Czechs established the National Free-
Thinkers organization, and abandoned the policy of abstaining
from government involvement. They also witnessed Czech lands
suffer an economic crisis, with industrial, textile, glass, and sugar
production plummeting. An agricultural depression took hold

as one-third of the work force became unemployed. New political groups appeared, such as the All-Austrian Workers' Party and the Social Democratic Workers' Party.

International events also influenced political developments, as revolts against Turkish rule broke out in the Balkans while Russia warred with Turkey in 1878. The Czechs strongly backed the Slavs and Russians, with Rieger seeking French support for them as well. The Congress of Berlin, however, placed more Slavs under Austrian control, angering both Russians and Pan-Slavs, who sought to end the Austrian and Ottoman empires. The Dual Alliance of 1879 established a defensive alliance between the German and the Austro-Hungarian empires to ward off a possible attack from czarist Russia; three years later, Italy joined the new Triple Alliance that retained the German-Austro-Hungarian partnership.

At this stage, the Czech Lands remained, as William V. Wallace suggests, "a Slav island in a German sea," even lacking economic or social supremacy at home.[39] They also failed to possess a unified nationalist movement of the sort that had recently succeeded in other parts of Europe. Nevertheless, on returning to the Imperial Diet in Vienna, Czech representatives achieved certain successes, including the recognition of the Czech language alongside German—which continued to be used exclusively by top government agencies—in Bohemia and Moravia. In 1881, the University of Prague was split into Czech and German schools, while franchise restrictions were lessened.

Over the course of the next two decades, Czech lands experienced significant economic and social change as industrialization quickened (one-third of the empire's rail lines were installed there), the population increased sharply, and urbanization similarly intensified. The ranks of the middle class expanded, particularly in Prague, while agricultural employment continued to be important outside that leading urban center. Economic disparities heightened, ensuring that class-based tensions would as well. German–Czech animosity complicated matters further, with Czechs often remaining in subservient positions, whether in large industrial concerns or in craft work. Czechs were increasingly resentful that their economic circumstances appeared tied to the dearth of political power they possessed within the empire as a whole. For many, working conditions proved difficult, with long hours, low wages, and recurrent unemployment.

The Bismarck government, to ward off the threat posed by socialists, implemented an industrial welfare program, which included social security laws offering state benefits to the infirm, the victims of industrial accidents, and the elderly. Czechs, for their part, also received greater representation, which led Germans, in the mid-1880s, to adopt their own policy of absention.

That same period witnessed difficult economic times in the agricultural sector, as farmers, who were directing larger operations, and peasants, who were cultivating beet and corn crops, suffered the most and demanded political action. Diet members aligned with the Old Czechs and the Young Czechs helped to establish a Czech Club, forming a new kind of arbitrary border. But the Young Czechs were determined to end the political challenge posed by their erstwhile allies. They formed an Independent Czech Club in 1888 and joined with disgruntled farmers to form a potent political force, soon sweeping provincial Diet elections. The displeased Franz Josef nurtured a compromise involving the Old Czechs and German Liberals, which resulted in both Czech and German educational and agricultural boards. The imperial elections of 1891 proved crushing for the Old Czechs, as Czech nationalism became more potent and radical. When young people in Prague demonstrated against Franz Josef, imperial authorities imprisoned scores of them for extended periods.

Nevertheless, the Young Czechs, who demanded greater economic and political change, acquired greater popularity still, relying on another expansion of the franchise to virtually sweep the imperial elections of 1897; moreover, 11 Social Democrats won seats in the Czech Lands. The Young Czechs convinced

Tomas Masaryk, who founded the Czech People's Party in 1900. Masaryk favored gradual reform in the move for Czech independence and was Czechoslovakia's first president when it was created after World War I.

Prime Minister Kazimir Badeni to issue the Language Ordinances in April 1897, which afforded the Czech language equal footing in the higher civil service levels. Within four years, officials in both Bohemia and Moravia were compelled to demonstrate competence in both Czech and German. That in turn produced another outcry from Germans, leading Badeni to adopt repressive tactics that offended Christian Socialists and Social Democrats.

Franz Josef ousted Badeni and rescinded the Language

Ordinances, but he had to contend with new organizations: the Radical Progressive Party, the Radical State Rights Party, and the National Socialist Party (which had no connection to the party of the same name later associated with Adolf Hitler). More conservative groups formed too, including the Catholic National Party and the Christian Social Party. Considering themselves stymied by social, economic, and political practices that favored Germans, Czech activists outside the Social Democrats established the National Council in Prague in 1900. That same year, Tomas Masaryk helped to found the Czech People's Party, also known as the Realist Party. Like Palacky, Masaryk favored

TOMAS MASARYK

New Czech nationalist figures emerged in the late nineteenth century, none more important than Tomas Masaryk (1850–1937), who came from the small Moravian town of Hodonin, near the Slovakian border, and whose Slovak-born father had been a serf. Growing up in a liberal household, Masaryk received his earliest education from his mother, attended universities in Vienna and Leipzig, and married a young American woman from New York before completing his doctorate and becoming, in 1882, a professor of philosophy at Czech University in Prague. He soon helped to found a new, popular periodical, and was one of the key figures in the Realist group, which advocated wholesale reform.

After joining the Young Czech Party, Masaryk became disillusioned with it, demanding what he saw as a more radical and more honest perspective. He first served in the Austrian Parliament from 1891 to 1893, where he spoke out for the rights of Slavic minorities. Beginning in 1893, he became associated with the journal Nas doba (Our Age), and two years later he published The Czech Question, in which he contended that a Czech national program should be drawn from "humanism, nationality, constitutionality, social reform, education of the people." In 1898, his Social Question critically examined Marxism but insisted that tackling "the social question" afforded "the kernel and the only resolution of the Czech question," thereby only furthering his reputation as an independent thinker.

The following year, Masaryk helped to defend Leopold Hilsner, a young Jew gradual reform, while envisioning a tolerant, socially committed, rational, democratic state. Particularly fearing what he viewed as German despotism, Masaryk was little more taken with the Pan-Slavism associated with the Russian empire; instead, he considered the United States a model nation, with its generally Protestant and explicitly democratic makeup.

As the twentieth century opened, Czechs still lacked the state autonomy befitting a nation. They did possess "a very strong sense of common heritage and culture, common complaints and ambitions," notwithstanding divergent economic, social, and political perspectives.[40]

who had been accused of committing a ritual murder. His support of Hilsner was based on both humanitarian considerations and concern that the Czech nation would be viewed as reactionary, even antiquated. The case could be likened to the one involving the French Jew Alfred Dreyfus, which also demonstrated the growth of European anti-Semitism.

In 1900, Masaryk established the Czech People's Party, also called the Realist Party. Returning to the Austrian Parliament in 1907, Masaryk continued to build on his reputation as a defender of persecuted peoples, whether Slavic or Jewish. When World War I unfolded, he fled to Switzerland, then joined Eduard Benes in London to agitate for Czech independence and secure national boundaries. When establishment of the Republic of Czechoslovakia was proclaimed, Masaryk became the first president of the newly reconstituted state, which he was determined to sustain as an economically viable, democratic nation with carefully defined borders that would help safeguard Czechoslovakian autonomy. (Slavs, however, contended that he failed to provide the self-government earlier promised.)

A firm believer in the League of Nations, Masaryk watched with horror as Nazism enveloped Germany and threatened Central Europe. Suffering from ill-health and reasoning that a younger leader should take power, he resigned from his post in 1935, to be replaced by Benes. He died in 1937, a year before the infamous Munich Agreement was devised, through which Czechoslovakia's arbitrary borders were markedly diminished.

* Quoted in Sayer, *The Coasts of Bohemia*, pp. 145, 156.

In the first decade of the century, the population in Czech lands grew by 7.5 percent, despite the fact that Czech emigration to the United States mushroomed during the same period. Industrial developments similarly continued to advance, with greater reliance on electrical power, notable increases in productivity, and a turn to more sophisticated technology. Demand for both consumer goods and urban housing heightened.

At the same time, a series of recessions helped lead to repeated shortages and high levels of unemployment. Those developments in turn resulted in labor unrest, which was aggravated by the continued wage disparities Czech workers suffered in comparison to their German counterparts. In addition, the plight of poor peasants worsened, while professionals and civil servants considered themselves trapped by discriminatory practices. In contrast, some industrialists and bankers did well and were hardly adverse to remaining within the Habsburg Empire.

Altogether, however, discontent mounted, but Czechs remained divided on what they considered necessary to rectify the situation. The emperor Franz Josef frequently proposed that Czech and German lands be partitioned, but Czechs were in strong disagreement with this setting of arbitrary borders, believing it would transform and thereby weaken their sense of nationhood. Masaryk favored a federal approach, which would afford considerable autonomy to nationality groups. In contrast to Masaryk, who did not view the franchise as a panacea, the Social Democrats demanded the franchise but focused still more fully on strike activity, wages, and the cost of living. Increasingly, however, various political groups, including Masaryk's Realists, called for universal adult male suffrage, and the Austrian government agreed to grant it by December 1906. At the same time, the distribution of seats in the imperial and regional diets still favored Germans, much to the dismay of the Czechs.

Also little helping matters was Franz Josef's foreign policy, which appeared ill-disposed to Slavic interests. Austria-Hungary remained tied to Germany rather than France and Russia—long favorably viewed by Czechs—in a military alliance. However, recent German actions had led to the formation of a British-French-Russian entente (understanding), thus pulling the Czech-favored countries closer to the Germans. Then, in 1908, Austria-Hungary took control of Bosnia-Herzegovina, which appalled the Czechs, who now considered their own lands more threatened as the empire's arbitrary borders shifted once again.

Subsequent imperial moves also appeared to demonstrate a less conciliatory attitude to Slavs. An old ally of Masaryk, Karel Kramar, responded by favoring Neo-Slavism, which contended that the fate of Slavic states was indissoluble; to safeguard Slavic interests, he urged an alliance between Austria and Russia.

Avoiding a Pan-Slav (supporting political union by Slavs) approach of his own, Masaryk nevertheless wrestled with the Austrian regime, condemning both the false treason charges leveled at 53 Croats and fabricated government documents intended to discredit Serbo-Croat political figures. Still, Masaryk remained unconvinced that a breakaway from the empire would serve the interests of Czechs. Believing that the Czechs comprised a nation, he felt no need to demand independence and obtain statehood. "We want a federal Austria," he acknowledged instead. "We cannot be independent outside of Austria, next to a powerful Germany, having Germans on our territory."[41]

As of early 1914, even the Social Democrats were refusing to champion outright Czech independence. A recent party congress had stated, "Czech Social Democracy declares openly and with no reservation … that the Czech question, being that of the future of a nation with no consanguine people beyond the boundaries of this state to which it could attach itself, can be solved only within the framework of Austria." Many did, however, call for a restoration of "state rights" associated with the old Bohemian monarchy.[42]

From the failed Revolution of 1848 to the outbreak of World War I, Czech nationalists struggled to acquire more autonomy for Czech lands. They did so in the face of imperial antagonism, repression, and big-power machinations, but proved unable to develop a united approach to sustain Czech nationalism. They were forced to contend with shifting, sometimes arbitrarily drawn borders, designed, in effect, to prevent Czech nationhood. The practices of Austrian monarch Franz Josef changed too, depending on the empire's standing in relation to other European power blocs. At times the emperor adopted a more conciliatory approach, allowing for greater freedom for his Czech subjects; at other points, he demonstrated a readiness to dilute Czech nationalism, no matter if that required imprisonment, repressive legislation, ethnically rigged elections, and/or nonrepresentative parliaments. Still, by 1914, it was increasingly clear that Central Europe and the arbitrary borders that characterized it would not remain immune to the wave of nationalism sweeping across much of the globe.

4

The Czechs and World War I

World War I, which erupted in the summer of 1914, tore apart Austria-Hungary, led to a massive revolution in Russia, and brought about the overthrow of the kaiser in Germany—events that produced political and social transformation across Europe and the Middle East while inevitably revising arbitrary borders. The war sped up the timetable for the Czech and Slovak national movements, setting the stage for the formation of the Republic of Czechoslovakia, which was proclaimed in 1918.

Following the declaration of war on Serbia by the Austro-Hungarian regime on July 28, 1914, no great enthusiasm was displayed in the Czech lands. The Imperial Diet and local parliaments were suspended, along with civil rights. The Social Democratic Party expressed strong opposition to the war, denouncing it as capitalist- and imperialist-inspired. Arrests were forthcoming, press censorship enacted, and several individuals executed for purportedly passing around literature attacking Austria. A number of key figures—the first was a radical young attorney and journalist, Lev Sychrava—traveled to neutral Switzerland, seeking to transmit information about the Czech cause.

During the first weeks of the war, a delegation of Czechs visited Russian czar Nicholas II, conveying the desire that the "free and independent crown of St. Veneclas shine in the rays of the crown of the Romanovs." The Russian military commander, Grand Duke Nicholas, the czar's second cousin, drafted a letter to the "peoples of Austria-Hungary," expressing hope for their development, prosperity, and preservation of their ancestral "language and faith." Happily received in Bohemia, Czech residents envisioned liberation by Russian armies, with Karel Kramar, soon to be arrested himself, urging Czech political leaders to let Russians "do it for us alone."[43] Czech socialists, who considered czarist Russia a reactionary state, at the same time displayed no desire to fight the Russians; this was in stark contrast to many German and Austrian socialists who eagerly joined their national armies. Nevertheless, Czechs entered the French and Russian militaries, while Czech colonies appeared in Western Europe, agitating for Czech independence—a drive that would underscore the importance of arbitrary borders in the region. In Chicago, a Czech National Association emerged, determined to support the drive for Czech nationhood when the conflict ended. Slovak leaders, who had to contend with Hungarian overrule, proved more cautious about how to respond to the outbreak of warfare.

Soon, Tomas Masaryk—while maintaining contact with a political network known as the *Maffie* that was established in the Czech lands—headed the small band of Czechs seeking support from Western democracies. As it became increasingly evident that the war would be prolonged, Masaryk reasoned that the Central Powers (Germany, Austria-Hungary, and their allies) might suffer defeat, which would allow for the Czechs' emancipation, while Russia itself could end up in a weakened position. Masaryk now called for "the retention of the historical Czech lands," plus Slovakia, which had "never belonged to the St. Wenceslas Crown." While previously he had opposed positioning the nationalist program around "Bohemia's historical state rights," he now "based his program on Bohemia's state rights, called for the retention of historical boundaries," and discarded the notion of self-determination, according to Josef Kalvoda.[44] Due to the presence of German residents and dealings with Germany, Masaryk reasoned that the new state should abut Russia and should stand as a kingdom, something he believed most Czechs and Slovaks desired.

For over two decades, Masaryk had been seeking cooperation between Czechs and Slovaks, but he believed that liberation would not be possible without support from other states. In Paris, Masaryk teamed up with two disciples, the schoolteacher (and political figure) Eduard Benes and the Slovak astronomer Milan Rastislav Stefanik, who helped to agitate for Czech and Slovak independence. In mid-November 1915, these men, joined by Josef Durich, a member of the Imperial Diet, established the Czech Foreign Committee, which called for the setting up of an independent state for Czechs and Slovaks.

Durich's approach differed from Masaryk's, as he believed that Russia would liberate the Czech Lands. The following year, the committee was recast as the National Council of the Czech Lands. National Council members watched as ever-increasing numbers of Czech and Slovak soldiers deserted Franz Josef's army. They were also aware of the presence of Czech colonies in Russia, many of which desired to cement ties between a future Czech state and that great power. Durich traveled to Russia in mid-1916, where he met up with different factions of Czech émigrés, including those associated with the Alliance of the Czecho-Slovak Associations in Russia, as well their opponents. He informed the Russian government that most Czechs favored creation of an independent Czech state headed by the czar, who would also take on the crown of Czech king. Durich established a Czechoslovak National Council in Russia, which articulated a pro-Russian position.

The independence movement gained momentum, notwithstanding the conviction of Kramar, Alois Rasin, and two other leaders of the *Maffie* who had been charged with high treason and crimes against the Austrian state. The death sentences ordered for the defendants were viewed as demonstrating the basic incompatibility between Czech interests and those of the Austro-Hungarian empire. In addition, a firestorm of international criticism poured forth, with leading French and British political figures condemning the capital sentences and supporting Czech nationhood. Like the French, the Russians warned that the murder of Kramar would amount to "the chopping off the head" from the Czech nation.

In the United States, the Bohemian National Alliance and the Slovak League agreed to support the creation of a state where Czechs and Slovaks would be treated equally. Under the so-called Cleveland Agreement of October 1915, those organizations insisted on "independence of the Czech Lands and Slovakia, [and] the uniting of the Czech and Slovak nations in a federation of states," with full autonomy to be retained by Slovakia. In November 1915, the "Czech Committee Abroad"

In February 1917, pressure from liberal political reformers over everything from involvement in World War I to food shortages forced Russian Czar Nicolas II to abdicate the throne, as announced on the front page of the March 16, 1917, edition of the *New York Times*. Czech leaders hoped the success of the February Revolution would strengthen their case for self-determination and autonomy in the Czech lands.

called for "total Czech independence and the reunion of Bohemia, Moravia, and Slovakia under one government," while declaring that the Habsburgs had repeatedly failed to honor obligations to the Czech nation. The manifesto, signed by Masaryk and many other leading Czech nationalists, demanded "a completely independent Czechoslav state."[45]

Meeting with French prime minister Aristide Briand in February 1916, Masaryk urged the Allies to construct "their own Central Europe" with recast artificial boundaries, and to maintain an alliance with Russia, which the Czech state would help to maintain.[46] Some in Western Europe opposed the idea of Czech independence, fearing the possible Balkanization of the Austro-Hungarian empire or its takeover by the Russians. Indeed, British and French diplomats had early expressed such concerns, contending that Austria-Hungary should be held together. Others, including Robert W. Seton-Watson, editor of the *Times* of London, favored the birth of a "new Europe," requiring the breakup of both Austria-Hungary and Turkey to rein in German imperialism.[47] Seton-Watson particularly viewed Masaryk, with his pro-Western thrust, favorably. However, not all Czechs deferred to Masaryk, with the Union of Czech Deputies opposed to the support by the Entente (Britian, France, and Russia) for the emancipation of "Czecho-Slovaks," and insisting that "the Czech nation, as in the past, now, and in the future, sees its future and conditions for its development only under the Habsburg mace."[48]

The February 1917 revolution in Russia, which resulted in the czar's ouster, altered events altogether, both in the war and in the Czech Lands. On the one hand, says Victor S. Mamatey, Czech socialists could now act as "good socialists and Czech patriots all at the same time." At the same time, conservative Czech nationalists were displeased that their hopes for a "Slav imperium," headed by a Romanov monarch, had evaporated.[49] Durich's preeminence in Czech émigré circles in Russia ended, while Masaryk displayed a warmer attitude toward the new Russian government. Czech political leaders were in agreement that the Russian revolution helped to further the ideal of self-determination, which could only strengthen the case for greater autonomy for the Czech Lands. They were also pleased that the new Austro-Hungarian emperor, Charles, allowed the Reichstrat (Austrian parliament) to meet—something that had not occurred since the war began—and he appeared to adopt a more conciliatory approach toward both nationalists and socialists. When the parliament first convened, Frantisek Stanek, leader of the Czech deputies, affirmed loyalty to the emperor but expressed support for "natural rights of nations to self-determination," for Bohemia's "inalienable rights," and for the "union of all branches of the Czechoslovak nation into a democratic Bohemian state."[50]

Nevertheless, in a March 18, 1917, letter to Paul N. Miliukov, foreign minister of the Russian Provisional Government, Masaryk declared, "I can say in the name of our entire people that we are at your side…. The solution of the Slav problems is now assured … the reborn Russia will unite the Serbo-Croats with the Slovenes and liberate the Czechs and the Slovaks." Linked with France and Great Britain, Russia would, he said, "solve the old Eastern Question: they will bring about an organic unity of Europe with Asia and Africa. The great eastern republic will join in this policy aiming at a transformation of the world and of mankind." Indeed, the Provisional Government soon declared support for the "partitioning of Austria-Hungary [and] establishment of an independent Czechoslovak state." Sharply contrasting with British leaders, who supported equality only for the Bohemian Crown and Hungary within the Habsburg empire, Miliukov stated that "the formation of a Czechoslovak state will erect a barrier against the expansive designs entertained by Germany against the Slav countries."[51]

Such high hopes were soon dashed, however, following Miliukov's replacement by Alexander Kerensky. A visit to Petrograd convinced Masaryk that an exhausted Russia would eventually withdraw from the war. He did agree with the Provisional Government that a Czechoslovak Army Corps should be formed, with 30,000 of its soldiers assigned to France. In the meantime, Western diplomats generally stopped talking about the need to liberate the Czech Lands from foreign domination, although British foreign secretary A. J. Balfour expressed hope that the people inside the Austro-Hungarian empire would be "allowed to develop on their own lines."[52]

A manifesto by Czech intellectuals, issued in May 1917, exhorted Czech deputies to support "Czech rights and … demands in the most decisive and dedicated manner." The deputies responded on May 30, expressing support for "the transformation of the monarchy into a federal state of free and equal national states," and "the unification of all branches of the Czechoslovak nation into a democratic Czech state, including also the Slovak branch of the nation." On July 2, the emperor pardoned political prisoners, including over 700 Czechs, before letting Kramar and Rasin go ten days later. But the conciliatory gesture hardly helped to dampen nationalist fervor, as exemplified by the effusive response Kramar received on returning to Prague that October.[53]

Matters became more uncertain still following the Bolshevik Revolution on November 7, 1917, and the resulting civil war in Russia. Masaryk affirmed the neutrality of the Czechoslovak military units. However, Social Democratic soldiers supported "revolutionary war against Austria-Hungary" while expressing solidarity with the Czech nation and backing the fight for independence. A battle ensued with Czech Bolsheviks, who sought to take control of the Czechoslovak military forces. On February 7, 1918, Masaryk felt compelled to affirm that the Czechoslovak army remained committed to the "revolutionary struggle against Austria-Hungary and Germany."[54] As the Brest-Litovsk peace conference began, Czechs insisted on representation and issued the Epiphany Declaration, which demanded a peace that would "bring our nation full liberty.... Our nation asks for independence on the ground of its historical rights." That new nation would help

> contribute towards the new development of humanity on the basis of liberty and fraternity in a free competition with other free nations, which our nation hopes to accomplish in a sovereign, equal, democratic and socially just state of its own, built upon the equality of all its citizens within the historic boundaries of the Bohemian lands and of Slovakia, guaranteeing full and equal national rights to all minorities.[55]

Treaty negotiators ignored the Czech requests.

Then, following the signing of the Brest-Litovsk treaty of March 1918, which resulted in Russia's departure from the war, Masaryk agreed with the new Bolshevik government, headed by Vladimir Lenin, that Czechoslovak military units should be sent to Vladivostok before continuing their movement to the West. As matters turned out, those troops, which Masaryk sought to keep apart from Russia's internal struggles, remained in Siberia. Lenin's regime acknowledged the Austro-Hungarian empire's existence and a redrawn frontier that enabled Germany to control a vast expanse of Eastern European territory, quashing the nationalistic hopes of many.

Masaryk now headed for the United States to seek support for Czechoslovak independence. President Woodrow Wilson had earlier expressed his belief in the principle of self-determination

THE PARIS PEACE SETTLEMENT

Following the end of World War I, representatives from the Allied Powers and the Central Powers gathered in Paris to devise a peace settlement. Six separate treaties were produced, including those carved out with Germany, Austria, Hungary, Bulgaria, and Turkey. The agreements with Germany (the Treaty of Versailles,1919), Austria (the Treaty of St. Germain-en-Laye, 1919), and Hungary (the Treaty of Trianon, 1920) influenced the actual makeup and the establishment of arbitrary borders for Czechoslovakia. The Treaty of Versailles granted portions of East Silesia to Czechoslovakia, while the Treaty of St. Germain acknowledged the disintegration of the Habsburg empire and helped birth the independent states of Czechoslovakia, Poland, and Yugoslovia. The Treaty of Trianon ceded the Hungarian territories of Slovakia and Ruthenia to Czechoslovakia, thereby firming up its southern borders. This created a new arbitrary border, separating Hungary and Slovakia, which had long been considered part of the Hungarian empire.

The Paris Peace Settlement attempted, however imperfectly, to further the cause of national self-determination by constructing new arbitrary borders shaped by both history and ethnicity. Eduard Benes based the Czechoslovak claims to Bohemia, Moravia, and Silesia, contends Victor Mamatey, on "historic, economic, and strategic considerations." To justify the inclusion of Slovakia in the new Central European state, and to ward off potential Polish demands on Slovakian territory, Benes hoped to maintain the longstanding arbitrary border between Poland and Hungary. With regard to southern Slovakia, Benes could point to "no historic boundary," so he called for "a 'natural' boundary" pointing to the Danube and the Ipel rivers. The new nation-states established as a result of the Paris Peace Settlement were multinational, with Czechoslovakia containing many individuals of German origin in the Sudeten, others of Polish extract in Silesia, and still others of Hungarian ancestry in Ruthenia.

* Quoted in Mamatey, "The Establishment of the Republic," p. 35.

and called for a quick breakup of empires. However, shortly after the United States entered the war, Wilson apparently went out of his way to assure Austro-Hungarian emperor Charles that the United States had no desire to see the empire dismembered. Still, on January 8, 1918, as he delivered his Fourteen Points speech, Wilson urged that "the peoples of Austria-Hungary" be afforded "the fullest opportunity of autonomous development."

Obviously aware of the recent taking of a national oath by hundreds promising to fight for an independent Czechoslovak state and of large demonstrations in Prague, U.S. secretary of state Robert Lansing, on May 29, affirmed his government's "strong sympathy" for the "nationalistic aspirations of the Czecho-Slovaks and Jugo-Slavs for freedom."[56] England, France, and Italy soon endorsed Lansing's statement. Then, on June 19, Masaryk finally met with President Wilson, who wanted to call on the Czechoslovak army to help overthrow the Bolsheviks, an action the Czech leader was reluctant to support. During this same period, however, U.S. sympathy for the Czechs only surged as word was received of the Czechoslovak army's capture of a 5,000-mile-long railway, and adjacent cities, in Siberia. On June 29, the Czechoslovaks took control of Vladivostok, which they would soon turn over to the Allies.

The success of the Czechoslovak army heightened the prestige of the Czecho-Slovak National Council that was still based in Paris. The organization sought recognition of a Czechoslovak state, along with its recognition as that state's governmental body. Secretary of State Lansing had urged President Wilson to unequivocally recognize "an independent Poland, an independent Bohemia and an independent Southern Slav State." On June 29, 1918, the French government indicated to Benes its support for the establishment of an independent Czechoslovak state, headed by the Czecho-Slovak National Council. Within days, British secretary of foreign affairs Balfour seconded France's declaration.

On September 3, Secretary of State Lansing, who had continued to oppose delivering "full recognition to the Czecho-Slovaks as a sovereign nation," nevertheless offered U.S. backing for the

Council. Writing to Wilson on September 7, Masaryk conveyed appreciation for U.S. recognition of "the justice of our struggle for independence and national unity." When the two men met at the White House four days later, Wilson informed Masaryk that "especially by your armies, you have demonstrated that you insist on complete independence. We have merely recognized an accomplished fact."[57] Ironically, during this very same period, the Czechoslovak army was increasingly on the defensive in Siberia.

In late September 1918, Benes indicated that a provisional Czechoslovak government had been established. On October 12, four Czech deputies met with the emperor, demanding above all else the formation of a Czech national regime in Prague. Two days later, socialists called for a general strike to support the establishment of a republic. The French government, on October 15, recognized the provisional government. The next day, Charles delivered a manifesto allowing the Austrian portion of the empire to be federalized, something that nationalists like Masaryk had long sought. On October 18, Masaryk responded by issuing a declaration of independence. Writing on behalf of the Czech National Council, Masaryk declared, "We have been an independent State since the Seventh Century." Now, Czechs declined to remain tied to Austria-Hungary while also insisting on "the right of Bohemia to be reunited with her Slovak brethren of Slovakia, once part of our national State."

In an effort to reach out to the Americans, Masaryk asserted that "the ideals of modern democracy" had shaped "the ideals of our nation for centuries." Masaryk promised that the Czechoslovak state, with its redrawn arbitrary borders, would afford basic liberties to all, adopt separation of church and state, offer universal suffrage, provide gender-based equality, and deliver equal rights to national minorities. In his own response to the emperor, however, President Wilson indicated that the United States recognized the Masaryk-led National Council as "a *de facto* belligerent government."[58]

On October 27, the Austrian foreign minister informed

Wilson that Austria desired a separate peace and would recognize the rights of the various nationalities within the empire. The following day, Czech deputies indicated that Czech and Slovak lands had been separated from Austria-Hungary, and announced formation of the Czechoslovak Republic, while the National Committee took control of Prague. A kind of bloodless revolution occurred, with imperial officials ceding power to Czechoslovak nationalists. In early November, Benes began receiving invitations to attend meetings with Allied leaders, including some scheduled for Versailles, following the war's end. On November 14, days after the armistice ending the conflagration, the Provisional Constitution of the Czechoslovak Republic was promulgated, while Masaryk was elected president by the Revolutionary National Assembly.

World War I opened with most Czech nationalists, including Masaryk, wanting to remain inside the Austro-Hungarian empire but hoping that greater autonomy under a federal system would be forthcoming for both Czechs and Slovaks. Some Czech leaders believed that Western support was essential, while others looked east to Russia. As the war continued, Czechs realized it might be possible to achieve independence altogether. Increasingly, some began to refer to historic Bohemia, the St. Wenceslas (Czech) Crown, and full independence while tracking and sometimes participating in the cataclysmic events associated with the Great War, including the Russian Revolution and the dilution of Emperor Charles's power. As the war threatened to reshape the artificial boundaries of both empires and nationalities, Czech nationalists declared the formation of the Czechoslovak Republic, whose own borders would be both arbitrarily and historically grounded. Yet even as support from the Allies followed, the nature, scope, citizenship, and territorial makeup of that republic remained very much in question.

5

The Czechoslovak Republic

The announcement of the formation of the Czechoslovak Republic hardly ensured its emergence. Drawing on the principle of self-determination appealed to the Allies, particularly President Wilson, while the establishment of independent states suggested a means to maintain order in postwar Europe. Most important, those states, it was contended, would serve to create a *cordon sanitaire*, separating the new Bolshevik Russia from Germany, which had suffered a crushing defeat; thus, the Allies hoped to construct an arbitrary border against the revolutionary regime. As for Czechoslovakia, its territorial makeup appeared particularly ideal, with its own arbitrary borders based on natural frontiers that included the low mountains encircling both Bohemia and Moravia. The ethnic makeup of the new state, Allied statesman believed, needed to honor the ideal of national self-determination. Czechs made up just over 50 percent of the population, with Germans and Slovaks the second and third largest ethnic groups. It was believed that together, the linguistically compatible Czechs and Slovaks, with their high birthrates, would easily make up a majority of the nation's populace.

Before the early stages of the twentieth century, most Czechs had expressed only a cursory interest in Slovak affairs. However, just before the start of World War I, Czechs led by Karel Kalal began to discard that ambivalence, with Kalal arguing that "the future of the Czechs was bound up with that of the Slovaks." At that point, more Czechs than Slovaks appeared interested in the possibility of a union. Like the Czechs, the Slovaks proved little inclined to fight on behalf of the Austro-Hungarian empire during World War I. Slovakia too experienced martial law and censorship, and received support from groups abroad, particularly the Slovak League of America. By 1915, Masaryk was highlighting the need to unite Czechs and Slovaks, informing Sir Edward Grey, the British foreign secretary, that "[T]he Slovaks are Bohemians in spite of their using their dialect as their literary language."[59]

Masaryk and Eduard Benes worked with the Slovak

astronomer Milan Rastislav Stefanik, who had studied in Prague and served as a general in the French military, to establish the new state. As mentioned earlier, in October 1915, Czech and Slovak groups in the United States crafted the Cleveland Agreement, urging that a federal state be created, with the Czech Lands and Slovakia to retain territorial independence. In February 1916, Masaryk, Benes, and Stefanik founded the Czecho-Slovak National Council, which became a dominant force in the Czecho-Slovak resistance effort, and proceeded to form an army.

As of 1917, Italy was the Allied nation most adverse to Czecho-Slovak nationalist aspirations, possessing its own designs on Austro-Hungarian territory. When Italy suffered a series of military setbacks, Stefanik inked an accord with Vittorio Emanuele Orlando, the Italian premier, that set up a Czecho-Slovak military army of 75,000 men in Italy. Along with the fighting undertaken by Czecho-Slovak forces in Russia, the army in Italy helped to generate goodwill among the Allies.

In May 1918, Slovak leaders, drawing on the principle of self-determination, began insisting on a joint Czecho-Slovak state. Beginning in late June, Allied nations began recognizing the Czecho-Slovak National Council as the effective Czecho-Slovak government. On July 14, the Czecho-Slovak National Council was announced, along with the claim that it possessed the backing of the full "Czechoslovak" nation. When the council proclaimed the independence of Czechoslovakia on October 18, it charged that the Hungarian Magyars, who had ruled the Slovaks "in an indescribable manner of violence and cruel oppression of subjugated vassals have lost whatever moral and human rights to rule over anyone except themselves."[60] The Hungarian government attempted to convince the Slovaks to remain within the empire, but the National Council, which included the Slovak leader Vavro Srobar, agreed to the formation of the independent Czecho-Slovak state, although what that entailed remained uncertain.

While Czech nationalists quickly took control in the Czech

Lands, the transfer of power proved more difficult in Slovakia and was not completed for another 19 months. Thus, newly proclaimed Czechoslovakia lacked artificial boundaries clearly distinguishing it in a physical sense from the recently established Hungarian Republic, which initially attempted to retain possession of Slovakia and to construct a Slovak empire. The Magyar government helped to bring about a general strike by railroad workers in early February 1919 and demanded a plebiscite on the matter of Slovak independence. But simultaneously, the Magyars shipped factory equipment they dismantled in Slovakia, along with foodstuffs and raw materials, to Hungary.

Border issues continually arose, with the Czecho-Slovak government annexing lands considered by Foreign Minister Benes as essential for the state's economic and military well-being. Benes's proposals were largely supported by France's Marshall Ferdinand Foch, who had served as Allied commander-in-chief; that nation hoped the new republic would serve as "a barrier against future German expansion, Magyar revisionism, and Bolshevik threats."[61] With the Paris Peace Conference impending, Czecho-Slovak soldiers were sent to occupy Slovak territory to strengthen the new government's bargaining power. All the while, the situation in eastern Slovakia remained thorny, with Victor Dvortsak declaring establishment of what proved to be the short-lived Slovak Peoples' Republic. Germans in the Czech lands briefly attempted to set up a republic of their own, while in Ruthenia, different groups backed alignment with the Soviet Ukraine or Hungary.

In March 1919, the Paris Peace Conference established arbitrary boundaries for the Czechoslovakia Republic, accepting the historic Bohemia and Polish-Slovak borders; allowing for the incorporation of Ruthenia, which obtained a good deal of autonomy; and rejecting the claims to Lusatia and a corridor to Yugoslavia. President Masaryk was instructed to devise a reasonable border separating the new nation from Hungary; he called for the placement of the Czechoslovak frontier considerably north of the Danube, to allow Magyars to reside inside Hungary,

The Paris Peace Conference of 1919 (seated, from left): Vittorio Orlando of Italy, David Lloyd George of Britain, Georges Clemenceau of France, and Woodrow Wilson of the United States. Although Czechoslovakia was not represented at the conference, boundaries for the republic were established by its attendees.

in return for Czechoslovakia's receiving access to the river right across from Bratislava.

The newly proclaimed Hungarian Soviet Republic warred with Czechoslovakia, hoping to grab both Ruthenia and Slovakia. After several months of fighting and of shifting frontiers, the boundary largely reverted to the *status quo ante* through the Treaty of Trianon, with Czechoslovakia acquiring one additional town.

The new Czechoslovak Republic, with its newly established artificial borders, contained over 54,000 square miles, making it Europe's thirteenth largest state. According to the 1921 census, its population of over 13 million was the ninth largest in Europe. More than 8 million Czechs and Slovaks resided in the new nation, but so too did almost 4 million Germans, over 1 million Magyars, more than 400,000 Ukrainians and Russiana, and just under 170,000 Poles. The census also recorded that 354,000 Jews

EARLY SLOVAK HISTORY

Czechs and Slovaks possess different historical roots. Abutting Austria, Hungary, Ukraine, Poland, and Moravia, Slovakia covers an area of 49,000 square kilometers, situated in the center of Europe. It features forested mountains, including the western Carpathians, with the High Tatras and the Low Tatras, and the Slovak Ore Mountains, containing silver, quality iron ore, copper, magnesium, lead, and zinc. Slovakia's hilly terrain favors farming, but forestry and mining have thrived there too. Its main waterway is the Danube. The people speak Slovak, an Indo-European Slavic language. National minorities can be found in Slovakia, the largest among them the Magyar, Romanis, and Czechs. Smaller numbers of Ruthenians, Ukrainians, Germans, Moravians, and Poles are also present. All, except for the Magyars, Romanis, and Germans, are Slavic.

Celts arrived in Slovakia around 500 B.C., minting coins and constructing military settlements. Eventually, they were pushed aside by German and Roman forces, which battled for supremacy in the first two decades A.D. During Attila the Hun's reign (435–453), Slav tribes began arriving, forming the first permanent settlements.

The Slavs had to contend with the Avars, but became subjects of the kingdom of Samo, which battled against the Franks, during the early seventh century. Many historians contend, however, that Slovak history truly begins with the formation of the Great Moravian Empire, which existed from 830–906. The Hungarians became the next overlords, serving in that capacity for 1,000 years. Under Hungarian rule, the Slovaks experienced industrial development and trade while maintaining their language and culture.

The economy was crippled by Tatar invasions during the first half of the thirteenth century, which compelled Hungarians to welcome settlers, especially German artisans, to help revitalize mercantile pursuits. The fourteenth century witnessed the reign of the warlord Matus Cak over much of western Slovakia, while the next century saw the Hussites maintaining control until the Battle of Lipany in 1436.

The defeat of Hungary by Ottoman Turks in 1526 led Hungarian nobles to migrate to Slovakia. The Habsburgs became the rulers of Hungary, relocating the Hungarian capital to Bratislava. After the Turks were driven out of Central

Europe in the late seventeenth century, Bratislava no longer served as the imperial capital. The incessant wars with the Turks and the opening up of the Americas for mineral explorations resulted in difficult economic times for Slovakia. Conditions improved somewhat during the reigns of Maria Theresa and Joseph II, as educational and labor reforms were instituted, along with elementary education. During the nineteenth century, serfdom finally disappeared from Slovakia, and the economy rebounded, thanks to a thriving garment industry and mining.

Slovak nationalism began to mount during the latter stages of the eighteenth century as intellectuals contested Hungarian preeminence. Cultural nationalism surged forth during the 1840s, when Ludovit Stur, who favored Slovak unity, began devising a Slovak grammar derived from the peasantry. The revolution of 1848 resonated with Slovaks demanding an independent Slovak state within the Austrian Empire. The Magyar-led government eventually crushed the rebellion, with repression ensuing. Following the establishment of the Austro-Hungarian empire, the Hungarians engaged in a campaign of Magyarization, compelling the teaching of only the Hungarian language in schools, and grabbing large amounts of Slovak land.

Nevertheless, Slovak nationalists maintained their campaign, forming the Slovak National Party in 1861. They watched as Hungary constructed a new railroad system, most of it coursing through Slovakia, which stood with Budapest as Hungary's most important industrial centers. Conditions remained difficult for most Slovak workers, who toiled long hours; Slovak farmers endured still tougher circumstances, with starvation not uncommon and many forced to migrate.

Slovaks tracked the Russian-Turkish War in the last half of the 1880s, sympathizing with the southern Slavs, Serbs, and Bulgarians. Younger intellectuals, with a Catholic or liberal perspective, considered the Slovak National Party too pro-Russian. Another group joined Detvan, a Prague association that viewed Tomas Masaryk as an icon. Slovak laborers, for their part, joined the Social Democratic Party, which received an impetus from the Russian Revolution 1905. More and more, Slovaks, like other minorities within the Hungarian empire, agitated for universal suffrage. Hoping to quash nationalist sentiment, Hungarian officials resorted to repressive tactics, arresting key Slovak leaders.

could be found in Czechoslovakia. Nationalism still appeared to be a potent force, although conflict seemed stronger in the case of the Czechs and Germans than among the Slovaks and Magyars.

The Czechs appeared to be characterized, according to Vaclav L. Benes, by "tactics of compromise, caution, and moderation," with many supporting "the humanitarian ideals" associated with first Frantisek Palacky, and then Tomas Masaryk. Masaryk's followers belonged to the Hrad (Castle) group, which favored a European security system and moderate social reform. Czechoslovakia possessed three-quarters of the col-lapsed empire's industrial capacity, along with a high literacy rate and considerable urbanization. Class differences existed, but tended not to be sharply drawn, perhaps thanks to the absence of a native nobility. Economic disparities proved more marked in Catholic Slovakia, because of considerable poverty, low educational levels, and the tradition of Magyar feudalism and aristocracy.

A nationalization measure in late 1919 allowed for the takeover of more than 200 business firms. The constitution of 1920 deemed "Czechoslovak" as the official language of the new republic, and designated Slovaks as "state people," not members of a national minority.[62] Still, Slovaks demonstrated displeasure with the document, concerned that it created a unitary state and failed to acknowledge Slovakian identity; they feared ethnic sub-mersion in the face of Czechoslovakia's new arbitrary borders. The Catholic populist and priest, Andrej Hlinka, longtime head of the Slovak National Party, denounced the constitution while demanding legislative autonomy.

Political parties on the left performed well in the 1920 par-liamentary elections, the first ones taking place after the draft-ing of the constitution. However, those parties were splintered between socialists, Social Democrats, and various nationalities, among others, who possessed contrasting visions of arbitrary borders of an ideological nature. Marxists desired a class-based government rather than one that was ethnically determined.

Radicals envisioned a socialist state, something that more moderate elements hardly desired. Marxists heeded Vladimir Lenin's demand that socialist parties meet 21 conditions to enter the Communist International (COMINTERN) and battled with less radical forces for control of the Social Democratic Party, which held the largest number of seats in the Chamber of Deputies.

Eventually, the Czechoslovak Communist Party appeared. Following a failed general strike in late 1920, however, the momentum for a radical shift dissipated. In August 1921, the National Assembly passed the Law against Terror, to prevent force from being used to bring about political change. In a balancing act, the national legislature that same month approved of the Law on Workers' Committees, allowing such organizations to be formed by workers in larger enterprises. Nevertheless, analysts like John and Sylvia Crane agree that Masaryk's "ethical egalitarianism" appeared to triumph over Lenin's "revolutionary socialist path."[63]

In late 1921, the former Austro-Hungarian emperor Charles returned to Hungary in an effort to restore the Habsburg monarchy, leading to the mobilization of the Czechoslovak and Yugoslav armies. Clashes occurred between Czechs and Germans in the Sudetenland following the refusal of German recruits to accept Czech mobilization orders. However, the diplomatic skills displayed by newly appointed prime minister Benes, who continued to serve as foreign minister, convinced even many Sudeten Germans that the republic was not going to disappear. Indeed, moderate German forces demonstrated a willingness to participate in Czechoslovakia's political affairs, allowing for a reduction in tensions.

Czechoslovakia endured difficult economic times from 1922–1923, as well as a then-rare political assassination in early 1923, when Finance Minister Alois Rasin was murdered. This led to the passage of the Law for the Protection of the Republic, which was directed against Communists, the newly emerging Fascists, and other groups willing to resort to violence for political purposes. Improved economic circumstances occurred outside of

Slovakia and Ruthenia by 1924, allowing for passage of the Social Insurance Law, which established a progressive national health program. Such developments, along with the devising of the Locarno treaties in 1925, which stated that the setting of Germany's eastern border with Poland and Czechoslovakia must occur peacefully, further convinced many that the Czechoslovak Republic would not fade away. Greater stability soon enabled parties representing national minorities to join government coalitions.

By early 1927, General Rudolf Gajda, former chief of staff of the Czechoslovak army, headed the National Fascist Community, which was supported by anti-Hrad elements and influenced by those impressed with Benito Mussolini's strong-man governance in Italy. Fascism appeared to dig deeper roots in Slovakia and Ruthenia, although the right-wing Slovak Populist party, led by Professor Vojtech Tuka, largely remained a conservative clerical organization. In January 1927, Slovak populists, including Father Jozef Tiso, entered the cabinet. To the delight of Andrej Hlinka, the National Assembly established provincial assemblies in Bohemia, Moravia-Silesia, Slovakia, and Ruthenia. Also pleasing to the populists, Benes reached an accord with the Vatican in January 1928, which no longer placed Czechoslovak Catholics under the tutelage of a Hungarian archbishop.

Following a pair of heart attacks suffered by Antonin Svehla, who had chaired the Czech agrarian party and had become a leading nationalist capable of placating disparate political forces, the populist Jan Sramek, head of the largely Catholic Czechoslovak Populist Party, was named prime minister. A furor threatened to erupt in early 1928 when Tuka, now a member of the National Assembly, published an article falsely charging that a secret agreement would soon ensure the demise of Czechoslovak sovereignty in Slovakia. In 1929, the National Assembly removed Tuka's parliamentary immunity and he was tried for treason and military espionage; the latter charge was also leveled at Gajda. Both men were convicted, with Tuka receiving a lengthy prison sentence and Gajda a two-month stint, angering Hlinka and inducing Slovak populist ministers to resign from the cabinet.

During the latter stages of the 1920s, Czechoslovak agriculture began experiencing a crisis that greatly intensified following the collapse of the U.S. economy and the triggering of a worldwide depression. Czechoslovak industrial production suffered mightily, declining more than 40 percent. Wages dropped precipitously, unemployment soared, numerous small businesses went under, and Czechoslovakia experienced an unfavorable trade balance. Fortunately, the nation lacked external foes, with Czechoslovakia's multilateral diplomatic pacts, bolstered by France's series of alliances, apparently serving her and the recently devised arbitrary borders well.

With Masaryk still in office, Czechoslovak democracy seemed strong but the economic downturn proved particularly crippling to Sudeten businesses and to Slovakia and Ruthenia. Through 1933, unemployment continued to rise in Slovakia, reaching the level of one-third of its workforce. Workers responded with strikes and rallies, many spearheaded by the Communist Party, as 200,000 gathered in Prague alone at one stage. Employers locked out laborers, and government officials had to contend with refusals to pay taxes or cover debts. Violence often occurred, particularly in Slovakia and Ruthenia. Not helping matters was the hardened ideological stance of the Communist International, which demanded that socialist and Communist parties view social democracy as "social fascism." The Czechoslovak president was himself denounced as the leader of a Fascist state.

As the economic situation worsened, political tensions escalated in parliament too, with the National League, furtively backed by agrarian rightists, viciously attacking the Hrad. The Hrad responded by going after the leaders of the National League, including Gajda, who was again tried and imprisoned, and subsequently denied his parliamentary post. Hlinka's Slovak Populist party shifted further to the right, garnering greater support as it blamed Slovakia's economic difficulties on "godless,

Marxist-inspired, self-centered Czech policies."[64] The German National Party, which had bitterly opposed the creation of Czechoslovakia, also began acquiring larger public backing. So too did the German National Socialist Workers' Party, which adopted increasingly extremist positions, demanding a pan-German state that would include the Sudetenland and espousing an anti-Semitism that had previously been evidenced. The Christian Socialist Party also displayed greater hostility to the government, which it considered too left-wing and secular.

The Czechoslovak government was determined to respond to the threat it believed emanated from right-wing forces, acting in 1931 to forbid the wearing of paramilitary uniforms or public addresses by speakers who were members of the German Nazi Party. After moving the next year to disband groups like the National Socialist Students' League, the government charged their leaders with conspiring to overthrow the republic. In July 1933, the National Assembly authorized the closing down or suppression of newspapers considered "dangerous to the state."[65] On October 25, the government declared illegal the German Nationalist Socialist and the German National parties; the previous day, leaders of the two organizations had disbanded them. Far rightists, led by Konrad Heinlein, proceeded to form the Sudeten German Home Front, which followed the same program as the German Nationalist Socialist Party.

In May 1934, the National Assembly elected Masaryk to a fourth term as president of the republic. His only foe, the Communist Klement Gottwald, subsequently fled to Moscow, fearing that he would be arrested. Nevertheless, the Communist Party continued to be legal in Czechoslovakia, the only Central or Eastern European state where that was so. In the parliamentary elections held one year later, the Sudeten German Party received nearly 70 percent of the German vote in Czechoslovakia, thereby obtaining several seats in the Chamber of Deputies.

During this same period, the Communist Party became less overtly hostile to Masaryk, largely because of a change in the Soviet Union's foreign policy. Only weeks after France and the USSR inked a mutual assistance treaty in early May 1935, Czechoslovakia signed a similar pact with the Communist state, although one predicated on French assistance to Czechoslovakia. In August, the Communist International followed suit, proclaiming that the fight against fascism demanded a united front of anti-Fascist forces.

Suffering from a serious stroke, Masaryk, now 85 years old, resigned the presidency on December 14, 1935, with foreign minister Benes, backed by an anti-Fascist coalition, elected to replace him. Concerns about Heinlein's recent electoral success undoubtedly helped convince many to support Benes, who had served six terms as chairman of the League of Nations. By the mid-1930s, militarist Japan, Fascist Italy, and Nazi Germany threatened to tear apart the League's tenuous collective security system, thereby endangering the Czechoslovak Republic. The Czechoslovak government, which sharply increased defense spending, began establishing fortifications along its lengthy frontier with Germany and modernized its military forces. Seeking to overcome the recently devised Franco-Soviet-Czechoslovak alliance, Hitler moved into the demilitarized Rhineland. By 1936, Czechoslovakia established a Little Entente with Romania and Yugoslavia, but it fell apart later in the year. In November, Hitler and Mussolini declared the formation of the Rome-Berlin Axis, a designed ideological arbitrary border that threatened to ensnare Czechoslovakia and other Central or Eastern European states.

Earlier that year, Benes's government had acted to restrict frontier territory in the Sudetenland, started tracking various individuals, and indicated that those convicted of espionage would receive the death penalty. While the Communist leader Gottwald, having received an amnesty, came back from the Soviet Union, Heinlein began negotiating more directly with Nazi officials in Germany; he also traveled to England. In 1937, British foreign secretary Anthony Eden urged Benes to negotiate with both Heinlein and Hitler, who had denounced the treatment of Sudeten Germans. Benes reminded Eden that these Germans were actually treated more favorably than any other minority group in Central or Eastern Europe.

The announcement of the *Anschluss,* by which Hitler annexed Austria, on March 13, 1938, surprised Benes, whose painstaking efforts to fortify Czechoslovakia now appeared woefully inadequate. In addition, he confronted demands by Slovak populists for Slovak autonomy, as Hitler plotted to carry out Operation Green—the conquest of Czechoslovakia. By October 1938, pressured by supposed allies, Benes was forced to cede the Sudetenland. Implementation of the Munich Agreement sharply reduced the size of Czechoslovakia, setting new arbitrary borders that left the nation far more vulnerable to external threats, particularly involving German forces or their allies.

Tomas Masaryk and Eduard Benes, along with other Czech and Slovak nationalists, had struggled mightily to create a binational state, with expanded arbitrary borders, which welcomed minority groups in its midst. However, the very effort may well have been contradictory because of the retention of strong nationalistic feelings among the various groups within its borders. Czech and Slovak leaders had fought to create a moderate, democratic state, but had demonstrated a readiness to resort to restrictive practices on occasion to prevent the Czechoslovak nation from being torn apart. At the same time, they attempted to balance larger powers to their west and east while preventing a resurgence of imperial control, a Communist sweep, and a Fascist *putsch.* Difficult economic times heightened political tensions inside Czechoslovakia, which the emergence of Nazi Germany exacerbated even more. Ultimately, the central European state, like many others, proved too weak to withstand encroachments by Hitler's Germany, leading to the end of the First Republic.

6

The Second Republic and Nazi Rule

In surrendering the Sudetenland, Czechoslovakia also ceded to Germany "1213 aircraft, 2253 pieces of artillery, 501 anti-aircraft guns and 1966 anti-tank guns; 810 tanks; nearly two million pieces of small arms; more than one billion rounds of small arms ammunition and three million artillery shells," Rich Fawn reports.[66] This meant, as President Benes had warned Great Britain and France, that they would have to contend with German aggression without the assistance "of the best equipped, probably best trained, and certainly most determined army opposing the Nazi regime" in Central Europe.[67] Pressured by Berlin, Benes resigned on October 5, 1938, the same day that the Slovak People's Party declared Slovakia's autonomy. Benes appointed General Jan Syrovy to replace him.

In meeting with German government officials in Berlin, Czechoslovak representatives unhappily agreed to the carving out of new frontiers, which included the loss of "the German-language enclave of Svitavy between Bohemia and Moravia," Theodor Prochazka notes. That splintered the important railroad line connecting the state's western and eastern portions. Prochazka adds that "Bohemia and Moravia lost about 11,600 square miles," along with nearly 3.9 million inhabitants, including over 700,000 Czechs.[68] Despite the territorial gains acquired through the setting of new arbitrary borders, Hitler, on October 21, 1938, ordered Marshal Wilhelm Keitel to prepare for a surprise assault against Czechoslovakia.

Prague also experienced additional territorial setbacks as Hungary took control of southern Slovakia and Carpathia and Poland grabbed Tesin. Meeting with Hungarian representatives, Czechoslovak delegates quickly agreed to hand over a railroad station and a border town. Negotiations soon came to a standstill, with Budapest conducting a partial mobilization and seeking to stir up unrest in border areas. The Vienna Arbitration in November pushed the eastern border of Czechoslovakia further north, costing that state nearly 4,600 square miles of territory, almost 1 million inhabitants, and towns like Kosice and Uzhorod. Czechoslovakia did retain control of Ruthenia, which

Germany also desired. The Poles issued their own ultimatum to Prague, which agreed to evacuate the Tesin region. Poland gained two important industrial areas along with eight coal mines, steel and iron works, and 227,000 inhabitants, over half of whom were Czechs. Two small sections of northern Slovakia were ceded to Poland, to the dismay of Slovak nationalists.

In November, the dismembered state, possessing shrunken arbitrary borders that amounted to a mere 70 percent of its former territory, was renamed Czecho-Slovakia. It now lacked both defensible frontiers and its defense plants, while its midsection, dividing the Czech Lands and Slovakia, had been reduced to less than 40 miles. Economically, the situation was still more precarious because of the tremendous loss of industrial plants, natural resources, arable land, and trade. Unemployment soared, leading to mass emigration.

Politically, boundaries narrowed too, with only two parties emerging in the state's western section: the largely right-wing National Unity Party and the more left-oriented National Labor Party. In late December, the Communist Party was outlawed. The newly elected president, Dr. Emil Hacha, sought more conciliatory relations with Nazi Germany, relying on the policy of appeasement. Desires for autonomy mounted in Slovakia, whose people considered the republic to have failed them. The Slovak Populist Party flirted with new partnerships involving Poland, Hungary, and Bohemia in various combinations. Ultimately, the Populists joined with the agrarians, setting up a new government in Slovakia, headed by Father Jozef Tiso. That regime outlawed both Communist and socialist organizations, and compelled all parties to join the right-wing Slovak National Unity Party.

Increasingly, Hitler plotted the destruction of Czecho-Slovakia. Responding to British and French inquiries, he declared on February 28, 1939, that Central Europe resided "first and foremost within the sphere of the most important interests of the German Reich." German leaders exhorted the Slovaks to withdraw from the Second Republic. Hitler himself told Tiso on

March 13, "The question is whether Slovakia wishes independence or not."[69] The next day, the Slovak Diet issued Slovakia's independence, with Tiso proclaimed prime minister. Hungary, having received a go-ahead from Hitler, occupied Ruthenia, even though its leader, Augustin Volosin, had declared independence in an effort to ensure German protection; now, however, Hitler had no interest in the region. On March 15, German forces entered Bohemia and Moravia; the following day, Hitler went to Prague, where he declared the territory of Bohemia and Moravia a German protectorate, bringing the Second Republic to an inglorious end. Subsequently, as John and Sylvia Crane report, "the formerly democratic republic of Czechoslovakia was turned into a territorially mutilated, indefensible, and economic and political fascist corporate state." Now, British prime minister Neville Chamberlain responded by declaring the Munich Agreement null and void because the guarantees regarding Czechoslovakia's territorial integrity lacked "any validity" due to Hitler's "unprovoked aggression."[70]

Overseas in the United States at the time of the German invasion, Eduard Benes responded to the news by declaring that the First Republic still existed. Now believing that Czechoslovakia had relied too much on Great Britain and France, Benes began seeking support from both the United States and the Soviet Union. He also called for the League of Nations to resort to collective security to restore the Czechoslovak Republic.

Returning to London, Benes reached out to resistance groups, which eventually formed UVOD (London Government Resistance). General Alois Elias, the new Czech prime minister, became the most important liaison uniting Benes's allies and the UVOD. Back home, Elias did his best to mitigate the anti-Semitic operations associated with General Rudolf Gajda and the Nazi roundup of Jews in Bohemia.

Nevertheless, the Nazi takeover of the Czech Lands threatened to become complete. Limited early resistance was quickly quashed, while Communists and German refugees from Hitler's Germany suffered arrests and deportations. Following the signing of a nonaggression pact with the Soviet Union in August 1939, Germany expanded trade with the Communist state, which resulted in employment and helped to prevent of greater opposition by the Czechs. While making it profitable for various businessmen and financiers to collaborate with the regime, the Nazis acted to silence Czech intellectuals.

After the Nazi-Soviet pact was announced, Benes sought assistance from the French, signing a treaty in early October that allowed the Czechoslovak army to conduct operations in France. The following month, the Czechoslovak National Committee appeared in Paris and was recognized by the French government. In December, a National Committee was set up in London, demanding a restoration of the Czechoslovak Republic, the return of lands taken by Hungary, and the reincorporation of the Sudetenland. When France fell in June 1940, its National Committee relocated to London.

By July, the Czechslovak provisional government-in-exile, headed by Benes, emerged, seeking international support. Shortly after Germany military forces invaded the Soviet Union the following June, the British government recognized Benes's provisional government. In late July, the U.S. government declared "its support of the national aspirations of the people of Czechoslovakia under the Presidency of Dr. Benes." That same month, the Soviet Union restored diplomatic relations with Benes's government-in-exile and reactivated the earlier treaty of alliance. Britain's Foreign Office indicated that among its war aims was "the restoration of the independence of the Czechs and Slovaks," with a return to the arbitrary borders Czechoslovakia possessed following the end of World War I.[71]

The war years proved difficult for both the Czech lands and Slovakia, as the Nazis drove between 200,000 and 1 million people into forced labor in Germany, with more than twice as many Slovaks as Czechs suffering that fate. At home, industrial production was geared to assist the German war effort. The Germans also set out to obliterate "all vestiges of Czech culture and political values."[72] In 1939, Hitler shut down Czech

The aftermath of the 1942 massacre of the village of Lidice, where Hitler ordered the murder of all male inhabitants and the relocation of women and children to extermination camps, in retaliation for the assassination of Nazi leader Reinhard Heydrich. The Czech people suffered immensely during World War II at the hands of the Nazi Germans, who shut down schools, removed signs of Czech culture, relocated families, drove hundreds of thousands into forced labor, and murdered thousands more Jews and dissenters.

institutions of higher learning, viewing them as founts of resistance connected to Benes. Intellectual life, according to Gotthold Rhode, "was to be mercilessly exterminated."[73]

Massive relocations of Czech families took place in Moravia and Bohemia to accommodate displaced Germans, who departed from Bessarabia and Bukovina. One of the top Nazi leaders, Reinhard Heydrich, oversaw Reich control of Czechoslovakia, declaring a state of emergency in several districts and ordering that Premier Elias be tried for treason. By late 1941, death sentences had been meted out to several Czechs accused of organizing resistance, including a pair of former generals. Eventually, Heydrich established stringent anti-Jewish laws, but an assassination team targeted him. On May 27, 1942, a pair of bombs severely wounded Heydrich, who died shortly thereafter.

In retaliation, Hitler ordered the razing of the village of Lidice, the execution of all male inhabitants, and the driving of women and children into extermination camps. That summer several other horrific reprisals took place, with some 30,000 murdered. The number of Jews slaughtered steadily mounted, with 56,000 killed from March–August 1942. Altogether, more than 70,000 Jews in the former Czechoslovakia were slated for extermination.

Although the resistance movement suffered grievously during this period, the fate of Lidice drew greater international attention to Czechoslovakia. On June 19, 1942, the Soviet Union declared that it recognized the territorial boundaries of pre-Munich Czechoslovakia. Later that year, U.S. president Franklin D. Roosevelt's administration affirmed his country's recognition of the Czechoslovak government-in-exile. The following May, Roosevelt hosted Benes at the White House. Benes was pleased to discover that the administration and the American public both appeared to favor "the existence of a strong and independent Czechoslovakia."[74] He also convinced Roosevelt to accept his proposal for transferring Germans out of Bohemia, Moravia, and East Prussia. Benes had come to believe that "the small Czechoslovak nation cannot live with a German revolver permanently against its breast."[75]

Benes also intended to strengthen his ties with the Soviet Union, something that Roosevelt and British prime minister Winston Churchill too considered to be necessary. Eventually, Benes signed a 20-year treaty with the Soviet Union, which he recognized would "be the principal factor in the new Europe." Inside the Protectorate, non-Communist and Communist forces jockeyed for position, anticipating the eventual end of the war. Hatred of Germans deepened but Czechs remained largely passive, while in Slovakia, Communists began speaking about a Slovak Soviet Republic. Benes had long focused on the matter of rebuilding Czechoslovakia, but by 1943, he was forced to pay increasing attention to Slovakia. Several key political and military figures there promised Benes they could overthrow the government and restore Czechoslovak unity as it existed at the end of World War I. A number of younger agrarians, led by Jozef Lettrich, preferred dealing directly with the Communists.

As for the Communists, they understood that to influence developments in Slovakia they would have to relinquish calls for a Soviet republic. By December 1943, a new Slovak National Council envisioned a democratic Czech-Slovak state that would afford Czechs and Slovaks equality and conduct a foreign policy friendly to Slavic nations, particularly the Soviet Union. Jan Masaryk, son of the late Czech president, attempted to convince Great Britain and the United States that they "must now do something for Czechoslovakia to offset the influence the Russians might be expected to obtain." Still, in London, Benes indicated during a public address that "the Czechoslovaks had not in the past been afraid of Russia, faced as they were, by the constant German menace, and they did not believe that the Soviet Union today had any designs on their territory or their democratic way of life."[76]

By 1943, the Tiso regime in Slovakia appeared to be coming apart, maintaining control only by the threat of German military action. Benes accepted the Slovak National Council's program in March 1944, and he encouraged a military revolt, to be led by Jan Golian. In late August, the Slovak uprising began, with 50,000–60,000 soldiers and about one-third that number of partisans, along with many Slovakian civilians and small numbers of Allied soldiers, battling German forces. By the fall, the Germans swept across Slovakia, conducting mass reprisals, shipping thousands off to concentration camps and sending resistance leaders like Golian and General Rudolf Viest to Berlin to be executed. But before his capture, Viest had ordered his men to head for the mountains, where they encountered partisans and from which they engaged in guerrilla warfare against German soldiers.

Increasingly, the fate of the former Czechoslovakia appeared intertwined with the actions of the Soviet Union. Benes, who remained determined to reestablish Czechoslovakia's former borders, received reports in 1944 that the Soviets were backing a breakaway movement in Ruthenia.He was still more concerned about what happened to Slovakia, portions of which the Red Army had liberated.

A letter from Soviet premier Joseph Stalin, dated January 23, 1945, sought to assuage Benes's fears, while Stalin instructed Gottwald to defer to Benes as president of Czechoslovakia. During the same period, however, the Soviets pressured the Czechoslovak Provisional Government to recognize the Lublin Committee, made up of pro-Soviet individuals, as the Polish government. Still, on April 4, Benes and the Communists agreed to the Kosice Program, which promised general elections; avoided Marxist language but supported nationalization of various industries; saluted the Red Army; announced that a new Czech army, patterned after the Red Army, would appear; suggested a foreign policy predicated on close ties with the Soviet Union; called for good relations with other Slavic states; and hoped for favorable ties with the Western democracies.

On April 7, Benes declared the formation of a new government to be headed by Prime Minister Zdenek Fierlinger, a left-wing Social Democrat who had served as ambassador to the Soviet Union. In early May, spontaneous eruptions occurred in territory still held by the Germans, soon spreading to Prague, but the Germans managed to kill as many as 5,000 Czechs. On May 9, Soviet tanks appeared in Prague, with government officials arriving the next day. Benes reached Prague on May 16, 1945, to tremendous applause.

Immediately after the announcement of the Munich Agreement, Germany, Hungary, and Poland had begun making more demands on Czechoslovakia. Even the ceding of territory had failed to dampen Hitler's determination to redraw arbitrary borders in Central Europe by swallowing up the rest of the newly renamed Czecho-Slovakia. Following the March 1939 invasion of his homeland, Eduard Benes demonstrated a dogged commitment to nurturing resistance to Nazi control, with the ultimate intention of restoring Czechoslovakia to its pre-Munich borders.

Benes hoped to reestablish the nation-state envisioned at the end of World War I, and he worked to cultivate support of a reunified Czechoslovak state among both Western democracies and the Soviet Union, and in the Czech Lands and Slovakia. By 1942, the Allies began pledging support for Czech nationalism, while nationalists struggled to sustain the idea of Czechoslovak nationhood in the midst of a repressive state cobbled together by right-wing Czechs, Slovaks, and Germans. In the latter stages of the war, Benes again sent out feelers to the Allied powers to ensure the re-creation of Czechoslovakia, with its full borders.

7

The Third Republic and Communist Autocracy

As the liberation of the Czech Lands and Slovakia continued, spokesmen for Benes's government insisted in June 1945 that the borders be "occupied entirely for Czechoslovak troops," befitting "the sovereignty of the state."[77] With the undisciplined nature of some of the Russian soldiers proving worrisome, the Prague government expressly declared that foreign troops were not required to ensure internal security or to protect Czechoslovak borders.

Controversy arose over the Teschen District, which Czechoslovak troops occupied following liberation, then withdrew, with Poles taking over in early July. A series of border incidents also occurred. Prime Minister Fierlinger urged the Soviets to remove their troops, while the Czechoslovaks also sought to convince the United States to carry out a phased withdrawal. Benes's government did agree to another pact with Moscow, allowing the Soviet Union to take over sub-Carpathian Ruthenia.

Before the National Assembly convened, Benes, relying on emergency powers, issued a series of decrees to establish government control across the Czech Lands and Slovakia, which the events of the previous seven years had left economically bereft. Benes was forced to negotiate with the Slovak National Council, which proposed Slovakia's and Bohemia-Moravia's existence as federated states possessing individual government and diets. Prague would host the federal government and parliament. While Slovak Communist and democratic leaders helped to draft the proposal, Czech Communist and democratic parties opposed the plan, perhaps recalling the troublesome Second Republic. A compromise, the so-called First Prague Agreement, skirted away from federalism while guaranteeing Slovakia's autonomy. Promised general elections were delayed for a full year, but a National Assembly came into existence, quickly rubber-stamping scores of presidential decrees. A coalition government, which included eight Communists, emerged in October 1945.

Enthusiasm for widespread changes appeared to exist among

Eduard Benes served as president of Czechoslovakia from 1935 to 1938, in 1945 and again from 1946 to 1948. Benes, backed by an anti-fascist coalition, replaced Masaryk, who, after suffering from a severe stroke, resigned in 1935. Benes was overseas when the Nazis took control of Czechoslovakia but reached out from abroad to resistance groups to reclaim the country. Because of the heavily anti-communist stance of the United States, Benes cast his lot with the Russian communists in regaining Czechoslovakia, a choice that he lived to regret. Benes resigned the presidency in 1948.

the general populace. In line with Benes's wartime determination, the government prepared to transfer two-and-a-half million Germans from the Sudetenland and some 200,000 Magyars, largely from Slovakia. Many Czechs returned from Hungary. The government also confiscated property, including 270,000 farms situated on over 6 million acres held by Germans, Magyars, and Czech and Slovak collaborators. Large industries, insurance enterprises, and banks were nationalized, while progressive income taxation was implemented. Benes considered this in keeping with the general trend in Europe toward socialism.

As 1946 opened, economic conditions remained bleak, with hunger threatening many. Soviet troops had recently departed, but the mass transfer of the Sudeten Germans had yet to take place. Coal shortages led to a slowdown in production, and rail transportation lagged considerably behind prewar levels. Aid packages were forthcoming, pouring into Czechoslovakia, thanks to such organizations as the American Red Cross and the United Nations Relief and Rehabilitation Administration.

Also early in 1946, treason trials began, with over 1,600 verdicts eventually delivered, including 150 sentences calling for life imprisonment or the death penalty. Shortly after the trials opened, several American soldiers, who were led by a German prisoner of war, uncovered top-level state records and damning documents secreted away inside Prague that pointed to Czech collaborators and Gestapo tactics. The American action had taken place without Czechoslovak knowledge and threatened to sully diplomatic relations until apologies were delivered, along with Benes's own records.

The hardline anti-Communist stance of Laurence Steinhardt, U.S. ambassador to Czechoslovakia, also troubled Benes's government, which desperately sought reconstruction aid. Reducing the amounts requested, Steinhardt justified his actions by arguing that American economic assistance to governments that contained Communists was counterproductive to U.S. interests. By contrast, the new Labour government in Great Britain sought to curry good relations with Czechoslovakia, while recognizing that close ties would necessarily exist between the Central European state and the Soviet Union.

The advent of the Cold War, largely pitting the United States against the Communist giant, dramatically impacted Czechoslovakia, which held general elections in late May 1946. The Communist Party outpolled any other in the Czech Lands, garnering more than 40 percent of the ballots, along with over 30 percent in Slovakia, where the Slovak Democratic Party received more than twice as many votes. British ambassador Phillip Nichols denied that Czechoslovakia resided behind the Iron Curtain, the symbolic arbitrary border in Europe Winston Churchill had recently insisted divided democratic nations from communist-controlled states. Thus, the Cold War witnessed the ushering in of a new kind of arbitrary border, coming on the heels of the territorial, ideological, and racial ones that Nazi Germany had attempted to construct.

After the newly devised National Assembly unanimously reelected Benes as president of the Third Republic, he selected a cabinet, which contained nine Communists, including party leader Klement Gottwald, who became prime minister. Concerned about the potency of the Slovak Democratic party in Slovakia, Gottwald was determined to end Slovak autonomy "even if we thereby violate national rights or promises or guarantees."[78] However, Gottwald also publicly declared that Czechoslovakia would endure no curbing of political liberties, and he indicated sufficient nationalization had already occurred. While the U.S. position toward Czechoslovakia only appeared to harden after the general elections, Nichols diligently strove to prevent the newly established republic from falling under the yoke of Soviet hegemony. But in mid-September 1946, the U.S. State Department halted both a credit to purchase American surplus war supplies, and negotiations regarding a $50 million credit through the Export-Import Bank to buy American machinery and raw materials.

The further intensification of the Cold War again dramatically affected Czechoslovakia, which hoped to benefit from the Marshall Plan involving massive reconstruction aid that U.S. Secretary of State George C. Marshall had offered in June 1947. The Czechoslovak cabinet unanimously voted to explore the possibility of requesting Marshall Plan funds, but a government delegation to Moscow received an ultimatum from Stalin to decide between East and West. Worried that any other decision would be viewed as hostile by the Soviet leadership, Benes's government soon recognized that it would not be able to take advantage of the Marshall Plan. In September, the Information Bureau of the Communist parties (Cominform) emerged, determined to cement Communist rule in Eastern Europe.

Relying on their control of the Ministry of the Interior and

KLEMENT GOTTWALD (1896–1953)

Klement Gottwald was born in the village of Dedice in southern Moravia on November 23, 1896, to a peasant woman, but never knew who his father was. At the age of 12, he went to Vienna to work with his uncle, a carpenter. At the age of 16, Gottwald joined the Social Democratic youth movement. In 1915, he began serving in the Austro-Hungarian military but deserted three years later. Employed as a carpenter after the war, he joined the Communist Party in 1921, soon writing for a series of Communist and workers' publications. In 1925, Gottwald joined the central committee of the Czechoslovak Communist Party (CCP); within three years, he became a member of the executive committee of Comintern (Communist International). In 1929, Gottwald was elected General Secretary of the CCP. That November, he was elected to the National Assembly, where he delivered a blistering address professing loyalty to Moscow and threatening his fellow parliamentarians.

Following Hitler's ascent to power, Gottwald adopted a united front approach dealing with Social Democrats, a policy that was criticized by party ideologues and which he attributed to others. By the mid-1930s, Comintern itself favored a Popular Front strategy to unite anti-fascist forces. With the outbreak of World War II, Gottwald fled to Moscow, where he later met up with Eduard Benes to devise a postwar strategy for Czechoslovakia, which both men were committed to reuniting through the restoration of previously existing arbitrary borders. In contrast to Benes, however, Gottwald hardly was adverse to the Soviet takeover of Ruthenia. In 1946, Gottwald became prime minister of Czechoslovakia, assuming the presidency after the Communist coup two years later. His reign proved highly authoritarian, with more than 200 deaths meted out to political foes, some 200,000 placed in prison or forced labor camps, and show trials conducted. The Stalinist tenor of his rule continued even after his death on March 14, 1953.

the police, Communists used charges of plots against Benes to arrest hundreds, including three Slovak Democratic Party members of the National Assembly. To dramatize their concerns about Communist actions, all non-Communist ministers resigned their posts on February 20, 1948. The Communists responded with what amounted to a coup d'etat but which they called the "Glorious February Revolution," shutting down opposition offices and newspapers, monopolizing radio transmission, relying on Communist-run police, and employing action committees to root democrats out of government agencies and factories.[79] On February 25, Benes appointed a new cabinet, selected by Gottwald, and withdrew to his country residence. He refused to call for armed resistance, fearing, as did Jan Masaryk, Soviet intervention. On March 10, Gottwald's regime announced that foreign minister Masaryk had committed suicide, leaping from the Czernin Palace. In June, Benes resigned, soon replaced as president by Gottwald.

The Czechoslovak Communists under Gottwald sought initially to carve out "a Czechoslovak road to socialism."[80] Instead they reworked the constitution and proclaimed their nation "a people's democracy," similar to those that had appeared throughout Eastern Europe after the war.[81] Communist control became pronounced, with censorship and religious persecution employed. Due to communism's greater appeal in the Czech Lands, Slovak Communists had to accept a subordinate position. Under Gottwald, nationalization intensified, along with sweeping land reform and a comprehensive program for social insurance. As the Cold War again deepened, with Stalin and Yugoslavia's Joseph Tito clashing by 1948, with the Soviet Union establishing the Council for Mutual Economic Assistance (Comecon) in 1949, and with the Korean War unfolding during the summer of 1950, Czechoslovak interests became more subordinated to those of the Soviet Union. As part of the Soviet bloc, Czechoslovakia joined Comecon and, six years later, the Warsaw Treaty Organization, designed as a counterweight to the anti-Communist North Atlantic Treaty Organization.

By 1948, the year of the Communist takeover, the Czechoslovak economy had rebounded, with industrial production surpassing that of 1937, before the Munich Agreement. The building industry continued to lag behind, industrial employment remained at a lower level than before the war, and agricultural production suffered considerably. Under five-year plans associated with Communist rule, Czechoslovakia experienced a sharp increase in industrial production and the building trade, but the quality of goods produced troubled consumers.

Other economic difficulties appeared. Fuel, especially coal, proved hard to obtain; workers frequently failed to show up for their jobs; machinery often broke down; bureaucratic waste abounded; and newly established state farms failed to produce an anticipated spike in productivity.

Suffering from economic failures they had helped to bring about and pressured by Communist neighbors and the Soviet Union, the Czechoslovak Communists steadily resorted to the iron grip of repression. Despite efforts by the Catholic Church to avoid antagonizing Gottwald, his government began controlling church affairs and prevented communication with Rome. Church leaders who refused to take a loyalty oath suffered trials for conspiracy and espionage. Hardline regimes in Poland and Hungary wanted the communization of Czechoslovakia to deepen, with the USSR, following Yugoslavia's breakaway, demanding greater Stalinization throughout the Soviet bloc.

In Czechoslovakia, show trials, like those conducted in the Soviet Union, played out, involving many middle-class individuals and professionals, while the Ministry of National Security was established in 1950, helping to send tens of thousands to prison and labor camps. More than 200 individuals, after their conviction on largely trumped-up charges, were executed.

The purge eventually enveloped Communist circles, including former party general gecretary Rudolf Slansky. A show trial involving 14 top party officials—most of whom were Jews—occurred in 1952, with Slansky among the 11 who were hanged.

Most striking of all was how Stalinist terror bred "suspicion, fear, and hatred" for the police state.[82]

Even the deaths of Stalin and Gottwald in early 1953 failed to dampen the iron fist that characterized party rule in Czechoslovakia. Mild protest in Plzen, which followed the announcement of price increases in June, was violently suppressed. In April 1954, another trial occurred in Bratislava, involving leading Slovak Communists, including Gustav Husak. They received lengthy prison sentences in this last of the show trials in Communist-ruled Eastern Europe. Under General Secretary Antonin Novotny, Czechoslovakia experienced something of a thaw, particularly following premier Nikita Khrushchev's denunciation of Stalinist terrors at the Twentieth Party Congress of the Soviet Union in February 1956. That spring witnessed both a writers' congress, in which criticisms of party rule were at least hinted at, and public student demonstrations. As unrest threatened to erupt in Poland and resulted in the Hungarian revolution later that year, the Czechoslovak government maintained its stranglehold on power. Helping to mute visible discontent in Czechoslovakia was the general disillusionment with politics that the last two decades had helped to foster and the recent nature of the purge trials. William V. Wallace also suggests that "revolt in the Hungarian style was contrary to the Czechoslovak tradition," while its brutal suppression hardly indicated that such an overthrow of communist rule was possible.[83] Strikingly, Czechoslovakia continued to hold thousands of political prisoners.

Indeed, the Czechoslovak Communist party, which provided somewhat greater autonomy for Slovakia, reasserted doctrinaire policies, speeding up the pace of agrarian collectivization and heavy industry. The problems inherent in central planning, however, compelled party leaders to initiate economic reforms involving decentralization by early 1958. Nevertheless, the economy experienced a downturn that required a series of unpopular currency devaluations, while failing to produce consumer goods that might have mitigated the system's growing

Antonin Novotny, Czech communist leader from 1957–1968. Though Novotny was open to some change, his regime was characterized by repression and economic stagnation. He was deposed by a liberal majority in 1968 and replaced by Alexander Dubcek.

unpopularity. Novotny, who had taken on the title of president in late 1957, saw matters differently, trumpeting the new Constitution of July 1960 that proclaimed the existence of the Czechoslovakia Socialist Republic and cheered the attainment of "really existing socialism."[84] No matter, an economic crisis threatened to unfold, with the economy actually declining in 1961 and 1962, consumer goods continuing to be scarce, and demands for reform taking hold within party ranks. All this proved troubling to the general public, which had been induced to mute political desires in return for an anticipated economic bounty. Khrushchev himself had prophesied that the Communist states would catapult past the capitalist countries in the economic arena, but in Czechoslovakia, as in various other Eastern European countries, the easy predictions appeared to have been overly optimistic, just as earlier promises of political and cultural emancipation under communism had proven woefully utopian.

From the short-lived tenure of Czechoslovakia's Third Republic to the opening stages of the 1960s, Communists had insisted that long-standing arbitrary borders involving class, ethnicity, and culture would dissipate. The democratic possibilities inherent in Eduard Benes's rule, beginning in the latter stages of World War II, however, had collided with age-old constraints of a territorial, national, ideological, and even imperial-cast. As the Cold War atmosphere suffused Eastern Europe, Czechoslovakia hardly remained immune as toxic rhetorical battles occurred between the former partners in the wartime Grand Alliance. Steady U.S. hostility to the united front makeup of Benes's government, which contained several communist ministers, helped to drive Czechoslovakia into the Soviet camp even before the 1948 coup. That takeover destroyed the Third Republic, resulted in Benes's resignation and Masaryk's untimely death, probably through suicide, but hardly ushered in the socialist state that Communist leader Gottwald proclaimed. Instead, dictatorial rule enveloped both the Czech Lands and Slovakia, topped off by purge trials that resulted in the self-cannibalization of the highest rungs of the Communist Party. The deaths of Stalin and Gottwald failed to usher in much in the way of reform in Czechoslovakia, which continued to be characterized by Communist-rooted ideological barriers that resulted in economic, social, and political malaise. That development, in turn, increasingly produced demands for change, often triggered by cultural forces.

8

Reform
on the Path to
the Prague Spring

With the economy flagging, the USSR's Khrushchev apparently still supportive of de-Stalinization, and Slovak demands escalating, the momentum for reform inside Czechoslovakia continued. President Novotny turned to Professor Ota Sik, who, like Novotny, had suffered through the concentration camp at Mauthausen and who now headed the Economic Institute of the Czechoslovak Academy of Sciences, to explore the possibility of decentralizing the economy. As Kenneth N. Skoug Jr. notes, Novotny hoped to rely on science and technology to effect economic changes and thereby avoid political alterations. However, Sik, like other economic reformers, envisioned a greater emphasis on supply-and-demand forces involving consumers, while reasoning that economic reform had to be coupled with political liberalization. In 1964, the Czechoslovak Communist Party approved of Sik's basic principles pertaining to economic transformation. It would be longer still until Sik's ideas were implemented to a certain extent, with limited market developments instituted in early 1967. Changes also occurred in the agrarian sector, with central planning reduced and a weak market system employed.

Political reform was also increasingly demanded. In fact, calls to reexamine the purge trials dated back to the mid-fifties, with a government-appointed commission of inquiry having declared in 1957 that only 50 verdicts would be tossed aside, and another 21 reduced, out of nearly 7,000 cases. A partial amnesty was declared in April 1960, when nearly 9,000 political prisoners were still held in Czechoslovakia. The Communist Party's Twelfth Congress in December 1962 revealed that a commission was carefully investigating the trials. The commission exonerated many purge victims and helped to free those still imprisoned.

The decision, which troubled Novotny, who had participated extensively in the purges, demonstrated that divisions existed at the party's highest levels. The commission was headed by Drahomir Kolder and included Alexander Dubcek, neither of whom had had anything to do with the purges; Novotny moved to control the commission's findings.

While some, including Gustav Husak, were rehabilitated, Slansky and four key colleagues continued to be denied reentry into the party, albeit posthumously. Other political changes proved necessary, resulting in the passage of laws improving the investigative and judicial systems. In 1964, Novotny empowered the National Assembly to serve as a genuine legislative body that would meet regularly and for lengthier sessions, consider legislation and query government ministers, examine regulations and their enforcement, and garner public interest regarding its operations. However, the Communist Party continued to select National Assembly representatives.

Also confronting discontent in Slovakia, Novotny responded by naming Dubcek, recognized as a moderate Slovak, to the Communist Party's Presidium, and by appointing Jozef Lenart, another Slovak, as premier. Lenart implemented the proposals for economic reform associated with Sik, which Dubcek also began to favor. Initially viewed as a moderate figure, Dubcek became more convinced of the need for economic decentralization and market developments, thanks to the antagonism of Novotny, advocacy by Sik, and the needs of Slovakia. In the first years of the 1960s, Slovakia actually performed better in both the industrial and agricultural sectors than did the Czech Lands. However, Dubcek and other Slovaks believed Slovakia should be experiencing greater economic growth, given that it initially possessed a weaker economic foundation during the early Communist era.

The Thirteenth Party Congress, held in 1966 and attended by the USSR's Leonid Brezhnev, who was general secretary of the Soviet Communist Party, highlighted the need to couple centralism with democracy. Having recently pledged "fundamental" economic change, Notvotny now promised "to put the management of our whole society on a scientific basis," and declared, "We must see that qualified experts are won over to the party."[85]

Speaking at the congress, Sik asserted that economic reform must be matched by political liberalization. That fall, Novotny called for a committee of the Institute of State and Law to undertake an extensive examination of politics under socialist rule. Chaired by the attorney Zdenek Mlynar, the committee included a number of Communist academics, who were determined to examine different systems, to ensure widespread participation of interest groups, and to guarantee democratic policymaking.

Other signs of change continued to appear, undoubtedly to the chagrin of Novotny's regime. Both intellectuals and young people appeared increasingly restless. At the Second Writers' Congress, which occurred shortly following Khrushchev's revelations at the Soviet Communist Party's Twentieth General Congress, the poet Jaroslav Seifert urged his fellow writers to serve as Czechoslovakia's conscience, and to be guided by a quest for truth and service to humanity, not by party dictates. Following Novotny's declaration six years later at the Twelfth Czechoslovak Communist Party Congress that the purge trials were undergoing reexamination, *Literarni noviny* (*Literary News*) and *Kulturny zivot* (*Cultural Life*), based in Prague and Bratislava respectively, began offering critical voices, contesting censorship and hidebound Communist ideology.

Other publications also offered new perspectives, while even party newspapers occasionally contained literature of a provocative sort. In 1963, participants at the Slovak writers' congress chafed at control by Minister of the Interior Karol Bacilek, leading to his replacement by Dubcek, who allowed freedom of expression through the journal *Kultury zivot*. On their own, the Slovak writers rehabilitated Ladislav Novomesky, yet another purge victim. The next month, the Third Congress of Czechoslovak authors criticized Novotny while insisting on freedom to travel and publish. For his part, the Jewish diplomat, Edvard Goldstucker, who had been let out of prison in 1955 and taught German literature in Prague, orchestrated a conference intended to resuscitate the reputation of Franz Kafka, the Jewish author from Prague, long viewed with disfavor by the Communist Party. Previously confiscated books returned to print, while the playwright Vaclav Havel began to publish works like *The Garden Party* (1963), which critically examined Czechoslovak society under communism.

Notwithstanding such promising signs and the apparent emergence of a youth-based counterculture, a kind of running battle with government censors continued. Enrollment by young people in government-sponsored organizations, including the Communist Party, plunged downward, with state officials acknowledging a "youth problem."[86] By 1966, small numbers of young people headed into Prague's Old Town, where they demanded freedom and democracy, resulting in the arrest and incarceration of a dozen students. While Czechoslovak writers condemned the treatment of Soviet writers like Andrei Sinyavsky, Yuli Daniel, and Alexandr Solzhenitsyn, government officials banned a series of publications, including *Tvar*, a non-communist literary journal; Havel served on *Tvar*'s editorial board.

The cultural divide proved all too obvious at the Fourth Writers' Congress, held in closed sessions in mid-1967. It occurred shortly after the Six Days' War, in which Israel defeated a number of its Arab neighbors and occupied land on the West Bank and along the Gaza Strip. Writers at the conference attacked what they perceived as the anti-Jewish nature of the government's position regarding the Middle Eastern conflict. The novelist Milan Kundera delivered the opening address, criticizing censorship and warning that the nation's literature threatened to amount to propaganda only. Jiri Hendrych, a member of the Presidium, angrily responded by blasting the United States and Israel, and warning that imperialists sought to destroy Czechoslovak socialism through "ideological erosion."[87] The dramatist Pavel Kohout defended Israel and pointed to Solzhenitsyn's challenge to Soviet censorship. On the conference's second day, Havel expressed his admiration for the Soviet writer's "true ethical stance" against communist autocracy. The novelist Ludvik Vaculik, to Hendrych's dismay, condemned the party hierarchy, the communist monopoly of power, and the lack of freedom. Bemoaning the loss of "so much moral and

April 5, 1968, *Time* magazine cover featuring Alexander Dubcek, who became leader of the Czech Communist party in 1968. Dubcek favored liberal reforms and continued the Prague Spring, pushing for even more "renewal" and "revival," which he felt was necessary to save socialism in Czechoslovakia. Dubcek eventually met with the displeasure of Communist Party leaders, including Leonid Brezhnev, especially after such reforms terminated censorship and allowed for spirited political discussion.

material strength," Vaculik, in a damning statement by an intellectual, indicated, "We have not contributed any original thoughts or good ideas to humanity."[88]

As word leaked out about the explosive nature of the writers' congress, Novotny attempted to quell the rising tide of discontent. In a public address on June 30, 1967, he declared that no deviation from Marxism-Leninism would be tolerated by his government. Within days, a trial of three dissidents began in Prague, with the writer Jan Benes subsequently receiving a five-year prison sentence, the lengthiest since the purges. Such treatment of literary critics hardly served Novotny well, nor did his handling of another crisis involving Slovakia. Now rehabilitated, Husak urged that Slovakia be granted genuine political autonomy. Dubcek's concern for economic reform led him to focus more on Slovakia's economic situation. More favorable discussion of federalism occurred, with some even talking about Slovakian independence.

Condemning "liberalism," Novotny, in early September, declared, "Our democracy is a class democracy." He promised to move against the "class enemy," while suggesting that personnel changes would get rid of "this conciliatory spirit, incubator of political compromise and inconsistency." Speaking before the Presidium, Novotny demanded a purge of party members who were not "one hundred percent sure" of the fight against the "class enemy."[89] Novotny attacked Sik while applauding purges taking place in other Communist states. At the Central Committee plenary sessions later that month, Novotny convinced his colleagues to expel various writers from the party and to reprimand figures like Kundera. Nevertheless, the nation's economic performance, as reform policies remained halting at best, also received sharp rebukes.

During meetings of the Central Committee in late October, Hendrych urged a hard-line approach to party control, but Dubcek supported reform overall, including inside the party. While Hendrych spoke of "socialist class consciousness," Dubcek countered with a warning that the "class epoch" could turn into a "smokescreen for conservatism and political sectarianism."[90] In response, Novotny blamed Dubcek for spurring nationalist sentiment among Slovaks.

Just before and during the Central Committee sessions, events involving young people in Prague resulted in public relations disasters for Novotny. On October 27, 1967, students had drawn the slogan, "We want freedom and democracy," along a river wall. Then, four days later, students from the Czechoslovak Technical College took to the streets after several power outages, initially in a lighthearted fashion, dancing and playing the guitar. Eventually, the crowd of 1,500 began shouting, "We want light. We want work."[91]Arrests ensued, leading to a sitdown by others and violence, landing a dozen students and three policemen in the hospital.

On December 5, the Dubcek Committee, appointed to examine Novotny's accusation about Dubcek's supposed nationalist deviation, dismissed the charge. Three days later, the USSR's Leonid Brezhnev arrived in Prague but took no position on who should assume power. Novotny resigned from the top party post on January 4, but not before threatening to resort to military action to remain in power. The next day, the 46-year-old Dubcek, viewed as a middle-of-the-road figure, became the Czechoslovak Communist Party first secretary.

The Central Committee acknowledged that "far greater encouragement of an open exchange of views" was required.[92] Invited to Moscow, Dubcek met with leading Politburo figures, who coldly listened to him discuss the need for "renewal" and "revival."[93] Dubcek also spoke with Hungary's Jan Kadar and Poland's Wladyslaw Gomulka, both of whom proved at best ambivalent regarding his insistence that Czechoslovakia undergo reform.

There, the resignation of Novotny from the top party post seemed to be liberating, planting additional seeds for what came to be known as the Prague Spring. Leading military figures, who were aligned with Novotny, lost their appointments. On January 21, 1968, a longtime party activist and purge victim, Josef Smrkovsky, in *Prace*, a trade union newspaper, called for the truth to be told "whether it be pleasant or not."[94] The Writers Union selected as its chairman Eduard Goldstuecker, with Jan

Prochazka, known for having defended both Tomas Masaryk and Czechoslovak authors in general, named vice chairman. The union pushed for Jan Benes's release from prison, which occurred two months later. The economist Sik went on television to explain that economic reform would benefit workers, something conservative party stalwarts denied.

In his public and party addresses, Dubcek suggested the mutual compatibility of socialism and democracy. At the same time, he recognized that the Czechoslovak Communist Party would not permit a return to "certain nonsocialist modes ... under the guise of democracy and rehabilitation."[95] Brezhnev and Soviet bloc leaders arrived in Prague to help celebrate 20 years of Communist rule. They listened uneasily to Dubcek discuss the need for large transformations in both the Czechoslovak Communist Party and Czechoslovak society, which required rehabilitating victims of the purges and working with intellectuals to democratize the party. The Czechoslovak government, Dubcek indicated, would move "toward a true invigoration and unification of all constructive and progressive forces in the republic.... This is the necessary prerequisite for a new inception of socialism." Regarding the party, Dubcek contended that its future demanded the nurturing of "democratic forms" evolving "from below," from laborers, intellectuals, and students.[96]

In March 1968, Smrkovsky orchestrated a pair of open forums in Prague for thousands of young people, where the problems of contemporary Czechoslovakia were explored. While many in the crowd appeared hostile to the Soviet Union, Smrkovsky asserted that relations were presently "built on the principle of equality, on the principle of sovereignty." *New York Times* correspondent Harry Schwartz later reported, "To a visitor to Prague in those days it seemed as if society was coming apart and reforming in a quite different pattern."[97]

On March 22, Novotny resigned as president, but in a meeting the next day in Dresden, East European leaders, including Brezhnev, warned Dubcek that he was "losing control" and permitting discussion that flirted with "counterrevolution."[98] One week later, the Czechoslovak National Assembly voted for an orthodox Communist, General Ludvik Svoboda, as president. The new makeup of the Presidium included progressives favoring reform, centrists, and old-line party members.

Also displeasing to the Soviet Union was the Central Committee's adoption in early April of reform measures, referred to as the Action Program. The reforms terminated censorship and allowed for spirited discussion about both present political possibilities and historical developments, including the purges. While acknowledging the dominant position held by the Communist Party, the Action Program underscored the need for rehabilitation of purge victims, intraparty democracy, relinquishment of a political monopoly, political freedoms, social welfare programs, a turn toward workers' councils in industry, and enhanced autonomy for Slovakia. The program did affirm that Czechoslovakia would line up with "socialist and democratic forces" against "world imperialism."[99]

East European leaders, particularly in Poland and East Germany, warily viewed the turn of events in Czechoslovakia, fearing they might lead to "counterrevolution" as had supposedly occurred in Hungary 12 years earlier.[100] Figures like Gomulka and East Germany's Walter Ulbricht remained determined to prevent "inimical, antisocial influences"—that is, "antisocialist" developments—from inducing a "spillover" in their own countries.[101]

By early May, the Soviet Politburo, headed by Brezhnev, was "united in the view that [the Action Program] is a harmful program, which is paving the way for the restoration of capitalism in Czechoslovakia." Brezhnev charged that Dubcek had "decapitated the party" by removing from positions of power so many "honest and committed Communists." The Soviet Politburo authorized the preparation of a Soviet invasionary force, under the code name Operation Danube. Soviet leaders feared that Czechoslovak reform efforts threatened the "gains of socialism" and the "common interests of world socialism."[102]

In contrast to the Soviet leader, Dubcek believed that rapid reform was essential to save socialism in Czechoslovakia. Indeed, the Prague Spring that he helped to usher in deliberately sought to bring about "socialism with a human face."[103] Support for Dubcek in Czechoslovakia appeared to mount, as exemplified by a massive gathering in Wenceslas Square on May Day, and by a large demonstration of young people in Old Town Square two days later.

Brezhnev summoned Dubcek and a number of Czechoslovak leaders to Moscow, where they were warned that their economic reforms benefited capitalism. Reports began to appear that Soviet troops stationed in Poland were heading toward the border with Czechoslovakia.

Nevertheless, President Svoboda proceeded to grant amnesty to over 500 political prisoners and close to 100,000 Czechoslovak expatriates. The National Assembly passed legislation allowing for appeals of prison sentences meted out since the Communist takeover in 1948. However, the Ministry of the Interior prohibited efforts to create new political parties, and Dubcek, worried about Soviet reaction, warned that free expression would have to be curbed. All the while, the momentum for still greater reform built up, as the Warsaw Pact staged maneuvers in Poland and Czechoslovakia during the summer. On June 26, 1968, the National Assembly passed a measure converting Czechoslovakia into a federation made up of the Czech Socialist Republic and the Slovak Socialist Republic; this reshaping of arbitrary borders, Kenneth N. Skoug Jr. suggests, recalled "the historic division between Czechs and Slovaks."[104] Consequently, it appears to be at odds with the Czechoslovak state created after World War I and the one that Benes had wanted to reestablish.

On June 27, Ludvik Vaculik published a manifesto, "Two Thousands Words to Workers, Farmers, Scientists, Artists and Everyone," signed by 70 others, which demanded more reforms and greater democratization. At the close of World War II, Vaculik acknowledged, "most of the nation welcomed the socialist program with high hopes." However, the Communist Party had dashed such hopes regarding an end to foreign domination and the creation of a society based on egalitarianism. "Retrograde" Communists, Vaculik continued, "still wield the instruments of power." However, support for "democratization" had soared among students, intellectuals, laborers, and dissident members of the party. Simultaneously, the possibility of "intervention" existed. Rather than cowering before the Warsaw Pact contingent, Vaculik declared, Czechoslovak citizens should seize the new "great opportunity" they had received. He continued: "Again we have the chance to take into our own hands our common cause."[105]

Brezhnev expressed outrage about the document, which Dubcek, at least to a certain extent, felt compelled to disavow, as did the National Assembly and the Party Presidium. By contrast, Czechoslovak citizens displayed greater affection for Vaculik's "Two Thousand Words" and Deputy Premier Sik maintained his efforts to sponsor economic reform.

In mid-July, Poland, East Germany, Hungary, Bulgaria, and the Soviet Union fired off the so-called "Warsaw Letter" to the Czechoslovak Party Central Committee, articulating what came to be known as the Brezhnev Doctrine:

> We cannot agree to have hostile forces push your country from the road to socialism and create a threat of severing Czechoslovakia from the socialist community.... This is something more than just your cause. It is the common cause of all Communist and workers parties and states united by alliance, cooperation and friendship.

The Czechoslovak government responded by pointed to its earlier rejection of the "Two Thousand Words" manifesto. It admitted that "remnants of anti-socialist forces" existed, but denied the charge that socialism itself was imperiled or that a change in Czechoslovakia's foreign policy was impending. [106] In no way placated, the Eastern bloc states responded with harsh rhetoric, charging that elements in Czechoslovakia sought to end the Communist Party's dominant position.

New maneuvers by Soviet bloc military forces, overseen by

Residents carrying a Czechoslovakian flag and throwing burning torches attempt to stop a Soviet tank in downtown Prague on August 21, 1968, as the Soviet-led invasion by Warsaw Pact armies crushed the "Prague Spring" reform. During the invasion, Dubcek and other Czech leaders were taken into custody. The resulting Moscow Protocol called for the ouster of reform-oriented officials, restoration of censorship, and retention of occupation forces.

the Warsaw Pact chief of staff, began in early August. On August 15, Dubcek insisted that Czechoslovak foreign policy was based on an alliance with the Soviet Union. Six days later, hundreds of thousands of soldiers from the Soviet Union, Poland, East Germany, Hungary, and Bulgaria took over Czechoslovakia. Both Rumania, under Nicolae Ceausescu, and Yugoslavia, led by Joseph Tito, condemned the invasion. During its early stages, Dubcek, Smrkovsky, prime minister Oldrich Cernik, and other proreform members of the Czechoslovak Communist Party

Politburo were taken into custody. Civilians mocked the invading soldiers and some initial efforts at passive resistance occurred, as Czechoslovak Radio continued to transmit messages calling for opposition to the occupation. As the popular resistance mounted, sometimes becoming violent, the National Assembly responded by condemning the invasion, demanding release of the imprisoned Czechoslovak leaders, urging defense of factories, and calling for a general strike. The Prague City Committee of the Communist Party also refused to submit, seeking backing from foreign Communists for what was deemed the first aggressive act by one Communist country against another.

Several organizations issued their own proclamations, damning the invasion and expressing support for Dubcek and President Svoboda. While urging calm, Svoboda indicated that the Czechoslovak government would insist on the immediate withdrawal of occupation forces. Soon, however, Svoboda was acting in a far more accommodating fashion to the Soviet Union.

Spirited off to Moscow, the interned Czechoslovak leaders watched as Svoboda and Gustav Husak negotiated a new pact, the Moscow Protocol, which Dubcek compared to the one drawn by Hitler in March 1939. Brezhnev informed Dubcek that Czechoslovakia would remain in the Soviet bloc, "with its borders the common ones of the socialist camp." As Brezhnev bristled, "We bought that territory at the cost of enormous sacrifices, and we shall never leave it."[107] Thus, the Soviet leader insisted on retaining the arbitrary borders—both geographical and ideological—that the Soviet Union had constructed. The Moscow Protocol signaled a wholesale departure from the Prague Spring, whose reforms were deemed counterrevolutionary; it called for the ouster of reform-oriented officials; reestablished censorship; and insisted on the retention of occupation forces.

For more than a decade, efforts to reform Czechoslovak society, culture, and economics had taken place, leading to the Prague Spring of 1968. Both inside the Communist Party and outside it, demands for a lightening of repressive practices occurred, with calls for the rehabilitation of purge victims, support for the opening up of the party to more critical perspectives, and insistence that the Stalinist path to socialism was hardly the only one or that which was most ideal. All along, the vast array of criticisms of Czechoslovak society was intended, in some fashion, to usher in what Alexander Dubcek eventually sought in the first several months of 1968: to humanize communism or, as he indicated, to bring about socialism with a human face. Such a determination, supported by various party leaders and many Czechoslovak citizens, however, challenged the hegemony held by the Soviet Union over Eastern European states. It also seemingly threatened the monopolistic hold on power Communist leaders possessed throughout the region. By late 1968, those concerns were grave enough to produce the massive invasion of Czechoslovakia, which again suffered the indignity of having its territorial boundaries violated. Thus, once more, ideological barriers, for the second time of a Communist nature, led to Czechoslovakia's borders being crossed in a determined effort to maintain arbitrary borders of a stringent cast.

9

Restoration of a Repressive State

Notwithstanding the Moscow Protocol, Alexander Dubcek, on returning to Czechoslovakia in late August 1968, hoped to sustain many of the reforms associated with the Prague Spring. However, the Soviet Union continually pressured the Czechoslovaks to reassert absolute Communist hegemony. Certain social and economic reforms could continue, but Moscow insisted that political barriers be put into place, with Soviet deputy foreign minister Vasili Kuznetzov remaining in Prague to oversee matters.

As the other foreign military forces departed, the Red Army failed to withdraw. Dubcek continued to refer to socialism's human face, writers printed a considerable amount of anti-Soviet literature, and Czechoslovak unions appeared vital. At the same time, the National Assembly approved of a press censorship law, supposedly designed to be temporary, and placed similar restrictions on freedom of assembly. The Soviet-influenced legislature thus sought to erect arbitrary borders involving political behavior.

Dubcek remained a target of both the Soviet Union and Czechoslovak collaborators, but he also retained supporters, as did the Prague Spring. In late October 1968, the National Assembly, to Dubcek's dismay, passed a measure dividing the Federal Assembly into a House of Nations, with both the Czech Lands and Slovakia to be equally represented, and a House of the People, determined by proportional representation. The National Assembly also set up a Czech National Council to rival the one that existed in Bratislava.

Public expressions denouncing the Soviet Union repeatedly occurred. On October 28, young people demonstrated for hours in Prague, crying out for the Russian soldiers to depart and demanding freedom. The next day, the police began beating demonstrators. On November 7, the police pummeled and water-hosed citizens who were singing the national anthem.

Still, opponents from both the Soviet Union and inside Czechoslovakia proved determined to further weaken Dubcek's position. As of early December, the *New York Times* indicated that Czechoslovakia remained the least shackled of the Soviet satellites. However, the Soviet Politburo soon moved to end the Czechoslovak resistance by going after Josef Smrkovsky, head of the National Assembly, and Dubcek. On January 7, 1969, the new Federal Assembly elected as its new leader Peter Colotka, considered far more compliant than Smrkovsky, who had warned that Czechoslovakia must remain unified in order to safeguard freedom. Even the self-immolation of Jan Palach, a philosophy student from Charles University who was bemoaning his nation's fate, and other protests failed to prevent the cessation of the previous year's reforms. Then, on April 17, Dubcek was forced to resign as the Czechoslovak Communist Party first secretary, while 11 members of Presidium, all considered to have supported the reform campaigns, were expelled.

The new Czechoslovak leader, the Slovak Gustav Husak, served as the Czechoslovak Communist Party general secretary for the next 18 years. A one-time purge victim and an early supporter of the Prague Spring, Husak had adopted a pro-Soviet stance after the invasion that seemingly served him well. Husak's tenure, initially referred to as the period of normalization, featured a return to repression and mass purges. Under Husak, half-a-million Czechoslovaks, approximately one-third of the party members, voluntarily departed from its ranks or were forced out. The Husak regime enacted stringent media controls, relied heavily on police surveillance and wiretapping, and meted out lengthy prison sentences for political prisoners.

Nevertheless, open opposition to Husak arose. The Ten Points Manifesto of August 21, 1969, condemned the ouster of Dubcek. Among its ten signatories were political operatives, journalists, and intellectuals, including Vaclav Havel. Addressed to Czechoslovakia's major political institutions, the Manifesto criticized normalization, condemned censorship, and insisted on the protection of human rights. Asserting that democratic practices should trump those guaranteeing the Communist Party a preferred position, the Manifesto also called for economic reform. At the same time, the document disclaimed any determination to attack the party, the state, socialism, or the Soviet Union.

Nevertheless, charges of subversion were eventually brought against all those who signed the Manifesto, but the trial was never held. A different kind of attack came by way of individuals associated with the Manifesto, for New Left students, led by Peter Uhl, dismissed it as "an avid lamentation, full of pathetic moralism and the typical naivete of a victim which brings law and good manners to the robbers' notice, hoping (my God!) that it will be enough to defend oneself."

The practitioners of normalization resorted to another tactic in an effort to discredit those associated with the Prague Spring. In a document titled "Lessons from the Crisis," the supporters of reform were said to represent "petty bourgeois elements and representatives of defeated bourgeoisie," often including the children of that privileged class.[108]

As the high hopes engendered by the reform campaign dissipated, Czechoslovakia experienced the federalization that Dubcek had feared. Increasingly, Slovaks appeared to garner greater representation in the political arena, with Husak ensuring that Slovaks obtained a disproportionate number of government and party jobs. Slovakia also did better economically than the Czech Lands, with more private housing, an improved standard of living, additional industrialization, and generous subsidies. Thus, over time, the Czech Lands appeared to be stagnant in comparison to Slovakia. However, the improved economic circumstances and opportunities, and even the political favoritism shown toward Slovaks, hardly placated them, for they considered Czechoslovakia to still be run by Prague.

With the passage of time, a growing number of Czechoslovaks, whether residing in the Czech Lands or Slovakia, appeared to withdraw from politics altogether. However, others, like Havel, sought to keep the spirit of the Prague Spring alive and resist normalization. Also among those determined to do so were students, workers, and intellectuals who sometimes operated through existing organizations, such as the Union of Film and Television Artists and the Coordinating Committee of Creative Unions, or who continued to associate with banned groups, like the Association of Former Political Prisoners or the Club of Committed Non-Party People. Strikingly, the largest group within the opposition ranks was made up of former Communists who were particularly prominent among the intelligentsia. Many had been dismissed from both the party and their jobs, with the more radical among them coming to favor popular action of some sort against the government. They were largely united in their belief in socialism of a reformist nature, the kind that the Prague Spring had promised to usher in.

The Socialist Movement of Czechoslovak Citizens delivered its first manifesto on October 28, 1970:

> Our struggle is political and positive. Neither violent terror nor sabotage are our methods…. We know what we want: a socialist political system in which political and non-political organisations will be partners, public and enterprise self-management, institutionally guaranteed control over power, and basic freedoms, including freedom of religion, as they were formulated among others in the Declaration of Human Rights which even this state has ratified.[109]

This movement received a boost when Polish workers walked off their jobs, leading to the fall of Wladyslaw Gomulka, one of Dubcek's harshest critics. Relying on the secret police, the government eventually responded by arresting the Socialist Movement's leaders, along with other figures linked with opposition to the regime. Referring to the ten trials that resulted, Husak declared in August 1972 that subversion had been thwarted. The suffocating atmosphere, exemplified by the annual arrests of hundreds for having purportedly committed political offenses against the state, only ensured that Czechoslovaks, by the tens of thousands, would continue to emigrate.

Concerned that normalization was not succeeding as expected, Soviet officials began reaching out to one of the heroes of the Prague Spring, Josef Smrkovsky, in early 1973, hinting that perhaps Husak-styled repression was too heavy-handed. Little came of this exchange before Smrkovsky's death in January 1974, although the Prague Spring champion had warned that normalization appeared to threaten détente, or the improved relations between East and West, that U.S. and Soviet leaders had been striving for. Meanwhile, the Socialist Movement of Czechoslovak Citizens headed in a new direction, indicating that political labels were unimportant and apparently discarding hope that communism in Czechoslovakia could be resuscitated. Nevertheless, the Movement highlighted the presence of political prisoners, the economic weaknesses of the present system, and the need to fuse democracy and socialism.

By the middle of the decade, the public expression of discontent with the Husak regime grew. In April 1975, Vaclav Havel presented an open letter to Husak, warning of mounting frustration in a society that was ruled by fear, coercion, and corruption. A group of dissidents asked Husak to mark the thirtieth anniversary of liberation from Nazi dominance by freeing all political prisoners. In late May 1975, Husak took over the presidency while remaining the Czechoslovak Communist party general secretary. Beginning in July of that year, the Helsinki Conference on Security and Cooperation in Europe emphasized the need for all governments to honor human rights. Other intellectuals complained about repressive tactics, while hoping that the promise of Eurocommunism, a democratized version of communism that proved most popular in Italy, might yet humanize communism. As international pressure increased, Husak's regime, in December 1976, released the last of the individuals who had been imprisoned during the sedition trials held four years earlier.

Then, in January 1977, the reform movement Charter 77, professing to represent different "convictions … faiths … professions" joined by a determination to sustain "civil and human rights," produced its first manifesto. Denying that it amounted to "any oppositional activity," Charter 77 desired "a constructive

Lech Walesa, the Polish shipyard worker and trade union leader who won the Nobel Peace Prize in 1983 for his efforts in organizing free trade unions and strikes that symbolized political freedom for Poland. Solidarity, the union launched September 17, 1980, was a victory against Poland's communist government. Walesa went on to become Poland's first freely elected president in 50 years. The situation in Poland caused the Communist Party in Czechoslovakia to tighten its grip even more severely.

dialogue with the political and state authorities," especially as it sought to highlight "individual cases where human rights have been violated."[110]

Containing over 200 signatures, the Charter described violations of human rights in Czechoslovakia and called for freedom of expression, the right to an education, freedom of information and public expression, and freedom of religious confession. The manifesto criticized infringements by the police amounting to arbitrary borders involving personal freedoms, including the right to travel outside Czechoslovakia.

Named as spokespersons for Charter 77 were the philosopher Jan Patocka, the political scientist Jiri Hajek, and Vaclav Havel. By year's end, over 800 individuals had affixed their signatures to the Charter, with a broad cross-section represented throughout the Czech Lands, but not in Slovakia.

Troubled by what Charter 77 represented, the Soviet government detained Havel before finally charging him with subversion, subsequently convicting him and three others. Havel received a 14-month sentence, which was suspended for three years. Arrested again in January 1978, Havel was released in March without charges having been officially filed. Affirming that he would never renounce Charter 77 or the moral duty to champion those suffering because of unlawfulness, Havel helped to found the Committee for the Defense of the Unjustly Persecuted (VONS). The next year, Havel and other leading members of VONS were arrested, again charged with subversion. This time, Havel was handed a four-and-a-half year sentence, while other leaders of Charter 77 and VONS also were incarcerated for extended periods. The repression intensified as Solidarity, the Polish labor union led by Lech Walesa, initiated a nationwide strike in 1980, for improved labor conditions and political freedom. Worrying about the contagious effect of the "Polish disease," which it feared might rekindle Charter 77, Husak's government clamped down yet again.[111]

Nevertheless, Charter 77 and Solidarity members delivered joint statements indicating support for the common determination to democratize their societies and to call attention to the plight of political prisoners. On occasion, hunger strikes were forthcoming, and, in Poland, at least, mass rallies. More and more, underground or *samizdat* publications were shared and seminal writings translated. In addition, Charter 77 members, beginning in 1981, undertook a dialogue with Western peace activists, emphasizing the need for human rights in addition to the removal of military occupation and weapons of mass destruction. By 1986, those forces coalesced to produce the memorandum, "Giving Real Life to the Helsinki Accords." Referring to the chasm dividing Europe, Jan Kavan notes, they contended that no peace would be forthcoming "without the eventual removal of this artificial barrier." By then, that artificial barrier had been in place for approximately four decades. Within a short while, Charter 77 members linked up with opposition forces in Poland, East Germany, and Hungary. On October 1986, over 100 dissidents from Czechoslovakia, East Germany, Hungary, and Poland signed the Declaration, affirming "joint determination to struggle for political democracy in our countries, their independence, pluralism based on the principles of self-management, peaceful reunification of divided Europe and its democratic integration, as well as for the rights of all minorities."[112]

The following August, opposition figures from Czechoslovakia and Poland furtively met along the border. They were in agreement regarding a set of beliefs also popular in certain circles in other Eastern European states. These dissidents called for the following:

> A deeper respect for social rights including the right to found independent trade unions; the ideal of political pluralism and self-government; spiritual, cultural and religious freedom and tolerance; respect for a national individuality and the rights of national minorities; the freedom to search for and create a better-functioning economic system which would provide a space for people's creativity and also grant all workers real responsibility for the results of their labor and their share of economic decision-making....[113]

The Eastern European dissidents began carefully following developments in the Soviet Union, where political alterations were taking place. Soviet general secretary Mikhail Gorbachev, chosen in March 1985 to head the country's Communist Party, initiated his programs of *perestroika*, requiring the dramatic reconstruction of Soviet society, and *glasnost*, demanding greater

CHARTER 77

After Gustav Husak replaced Alexander Dubcek as head of the Czechoslovak Communist Party in April 1969, nonviolent resistance unfolded, particularly in the Czech Lands. *Samizdat* writings emerged by the fall, and various organizations struggled to continue, despite being declared illegal. Mass purges occurred through 1971, affecting more than 500,000 individuals, including many intellectuals and other veterans of the Prague Spring. Resistance largely petered out by 1973 but within two years resurfaced as the Helsinki Conference on Security and Cooperation in Europe took place in the summer of 1975, highlighting the issue of human rights.

While others were clearly emboldened by Helsinki, the playwright Vaclav Havel had long demonstrated a willingness to challenge government authority. He joined with 200 other dissidents to produce Charter 77, which was signed January 1, 1977, and insisted on the defense of civil and human rights. The manifesto asserted that "freedoms and rights ... are important values of civilization for which many progressive people [have] been striving throughout history."

Thoroughly displeased with the direct and indirect criticisms contained in Charter 77, the Husak government targeted key figures in the movement, including Havel, for prosecution. A kind of tug-of-war ensued over the next several years, with the lengthy incarceration of Charter 77 leaders, efforts undertaken to clamp down on freedom of expression, and an embittered propaganda campaign waged against the signatories of the manifesto. Although fewer then 2,000 individuals openly expressed their allegiance to Charter 77, the movement managed to publish several hundred documents outside of Czechoslovakia attesting to the brutal nature of Husak's regime. Havel helped to create another organization, the Committee for the Defense of the Unjustly Persecuted (VONS), which recorded the histories of those persecuted by the government. Few suffered more than Havel himself, who was finally released shortly before his extended prison sentence was completed, because of a near fatal illness that threatened to convert him into a martyr for the movement.

*Quoted in Charter 77.

openness. Quickly, Gorbachev determined that such changes required *demokratizatsiaa*, or the democratization of the Soviet Union. Anticipating Gorbachev's visit to Prague in April 1987, Husak spoke of the need for *prestavba*, a Czechoslovak variety of *perestroika*. Little change was immediately forthcoming, but in December of that year, Husak resigned as Czechoslovak Communist Party general secretary, to be replaced by Milos Jakes. However, in contrast to Poland and Hungary, no groups in the party leadership proved desirous of genuine reform or of lightening the government's repressive hold on Czechoslovak society. Nevertheless, the forces of change, inside Czechoslovakia, the Soviet Union, and the rest of the Eastern bloc, continued to gather momentum.

The halting of the Prague Spring and the ouster of Alexander Dubcek's reform government failed to prevent the demand for reform in Czechoslovakia. The hard-line, neo-Stalinist regime of Gustav Husak, in an effort to reaffirm ideological hegemony of a near absolute sort, rolled back political changes associated with the Prague Spring and clamped down on political dissidents. Husak proved determined to turn the clock back, in a sense, to a period characterized by arbitrary borders of an ideological nature. Those associated with the opposition, including stalwart Prague Spring advocates, signatories of various protest manifestos, dissident Communists, and Charter 77 participants, proved equally committed, in their own fashion, to demonstrating that such borders need not be absolute.

10

The Velvet Revolution and its Aftermath

In March 1988, Vaclav Havel was again taken into custody, in the midst of public demonstrations calling for religious freedom marking the founding of the Czechoslovak republic 70 years earlier, and recalling the self-immolation of Jan Palach. Increasingly, Havel was viewed as the most important figure in the Czechoslovak human rights movement, in the very period when Mikhail Gorbachev affirmed that "equal rights and non-interference are becoming universally recognized rules of international relations."

On August 21, 1988, the twentieth anniversary of the Soviet invasion of Czechoslovakia, 10,000 demonstrators marched through Prague, heralding freedom. When the size of the demonstration waned, the police employed tear gas and batons to disperse those remaining in Old Town Square. On October 28, another demonstration occurred, with 5,000 gathering in Wenceslas Square, demanding "Freedom! Freedom!" which resulted in a quick, brutal response by police forces.[114]

Yet another public demonstration took place in Prague on December 10, the fortieth anniversary of the Universal Declaration of Human Rights. To the dismay of the government, well-known dissidents, including Havel, spoke at the gathering.

The government determined to clamp down more forcefully, as Palach Week, honoring the young man who had given his life on behalf of the nationalist struggle, began on January 15, 1989. Thousands again congregated in Prague, resulting in a massive, seemingly indiscriminate use of force by the police. Dissidents, including Havel, suffered arrest. Charged with incitement and obstruction, Havel received a nine-month prison sentence, but would be released after serving four months.

Worries about the situation in Czechoslovakia led to a strong condemnation of the demonstration, which appeared in *Pravda*, the Soviet Communist Party's newspaper. This was noteworthy, because Gorbachev's increased reliance on *perestroika*, *glasnost*, and *demokratizatsiaa* had helped to usher in dramatic changes throughout much of Eastern Europe. However, while Gorbachev renounced the Brezhnev Doctrine, which effectively promised a

Soviet invasion if Communist rule were endangered anywhere in the Eastern bloc, he still hoped to maintain the Soviet bloc; in other words, Gorbachev desired to keep in place the arbitrary borders that enabled the Soviet Union to possess something of an empire outside its own expansive boundaries.

Increasingly, however, Soviet hegemony, like the Communist monopolistic hold on power, appeared increasingly shaky. General Wojciech Jaruzelski, who had established martial rule in Poland, felt compelled to negotiate with the Solidarity labor

VACLAV HAVEL

Vaclav Havel was born on October 5, 1936, into an affluent, well-regarded family that resided in Prague. Refused admission into humanities programs for political reasons, Havel enrolled at the Economics Faculty of the Czech Technical College in Prague. In 1956, he met Olga Spilchalova, whom he eventually married.

An aspiring poet, Havel attended a three-day conference for young writers and cultural figures in the fall of 1956, as the Hungarian Revolution was playing out. Associated with Group 42, which challenged older writers, Havel spoke up, asking why those in attendance failed to support banned poets. Working as a stage technician, Havel began drafting his own plays, including *The Garden Party* (1963), which critically examined Czechoslovak society under Communist dominance.

Havel became convinced that every act suggesting social awareness helped to weaken the Communist system. A key figure in the Czechoslovak Writers' Union, Havel served on the literary board of the non-Communist publication *Tvar*, which the government soon shut down. He was determined to contest the ideological barrier resulting from Czechoslovak Communism.

Havel became intimately involved with the political, cultural, and intellectual flowering known as the Prague Spring, serving as chair of the Circle of Independent Writers. As Soviet tanks rolled through Czechoslovakia in August 1968, Havel warned that passive resistance alone would fail to end Communist tyranny. He signed a petition damning the ouster of Alexander Dubcek; this led to charges of subversion. While the trial was never held, the movement, while Jan Kadar, longtime First Secretary of the Hungarian Socialist Workers' Party and prime minister (1956–1998), had already relinquished his hold on power.

In Czechoslovakia, open letters protested the arrest of Havel and other top dissidents, and called for actions leading to a pluralist democracy. Hardly bolstering the government's position were the uncertain economic times Czechoslovakia was experiencing. Economists reasoned that production costs needed to be curbed to allow Czechoslovak products to become more

Writers' Union was shut down and Havel's work was effectively banned throughout Czechoslovakia.

In 1975, he fired off a note to President Gustav Husak, warning that frustration was mounting in the nation. In 1977, Havel became involved with the establishment of Charter 77, a human rights movement, and the Committee for the Defense of the Unjustly Persecuted (VONS). Eventually, convicted of subversion, Havel served nearly the entirety of a four-and-a-half year sentence before concerns about his health, and possible martyrdom, led authorities to release him. By 1988, Havel was considered the leading figure in the human rights campaign, and he was again criticizing the government's repressive ways. By early January 1989, Havel was back in prison but was let out after serving four months. In November, he helped to establish Civic Forum (CF), which became a key force in ushering in the nonviolent Velvet Revolution that felled the Communist regime and terminated its political barriers.

On December 29, 1989, the Federal Assembly elected Havel president of the republic. Reelected the following year, he helped to usher in the democratization of the former Communist state. Notwithstanding his great moral stature, however, Havel was unable to prevent the unraveling of the nation. In January 1993, he was chosen president of the new Czech Republic, which required new arbitrary borders. Remarried in 1996 following the death of his first wife, Havel was elected to another term in January 1998. When that term expired, Havel continued to champion human rights and to argue that "the value of freedom is linked with responsibility. And if freedom has no such responsibility associated with it, then it loses contents, it loses sense, and it also loses weight."

competitive, but that required structural changes, the introduction of still unacceptable market forces, and the likelihood of
politically unpopular high levels of unemployment.

Similar quandaries occurred in other Eastern European states,
while a flood of refugees began pouring forth, with East Germans
racing into Hungary in the summer of 1989, seeking transit to the
West. When Hungary opened its border to East German refugees,
additional thousands, many young and skilled, joined in a mass
departure. East Germany began experiencing massive demonstrations, and reformist forces inside the Communist party
ousted Erich Honecker, head of state since 1976, and attempted
to deliver concessions, including the right to travel freely.
Demands continued to surface, with calls for democracy and
reunification; all of this demonstrated the inherent weakness of
the arbitrary borders that had held the Iron Curtain in place. As
millions headed into West Germany, portions of the Berlin Wall,
that most graphic physical symbol of an artificial border spurred
by the Cold War, began to be ripped apart.

Czechoslovakia could hardly remain immune to the
crescendo of events enveloping Eastern Europe. Its hidebound
government appeared increasingly isolated, even inside the
Soviet bloc. By early November, as Bernard Wheaton and
Zdenek Kavan note, the Jakes regime ironically remained, in
effect, "the last bastion of conservatism in Central and Eastern
Europe."[115]Former dissidents now were stationed in government
posts in Poland. Watching events in nearby states undoubtedly
emboldened those determined to reform Czechoslovakia.

The government's legitimacy was further eroded by the
employment of massive police violence on November 17, 1989,
during a march commemorating the fiftieth anniversary of
Hitler's closure of Czech universities. As the crowd eventually
swelled to some 50,000, banners and speeches called for freedom,
democracy, *perestroika*, support for political prisoners, Jakes's
resignation, and resistance. Eventually, the police responded by
wielding truncheons against the heads of countless individuals,
with hundreds injured altogether.

A Czechoslovakian student rings a bell while holding a poster of Vaclav Havel during the Velvet Revolution in Prague, 1989. The Velvet Revolution, occurring simultaneously with Gorbachev's Soviet reforms of *perestroika*, *glasnost*, and *demokratizatsiaa*, provided a bloodless end to Communism in Czechoslovakia. Havel, a playwright whose leadership during the struggle proved instrumental in bringing about this revolution, was immediately elected president.

As word spread about the turn of events in Prague, calls for a student strike or a general strike emerged. Most significant of all, on November 19, dissidents established Citizens Forum (CF) in Prague and Public Against Violence (VPN) in Bratislava.

Citizens Forum, spearheaded by Havel, demanded the resignation of top members of the Communist Party's Central Committee, including Husak and Jakes. CF also insisted on an investigation of "the planned intervention of the five states of the Warsaw Pact in 1968," and the immediate release of "all prisoners of conscience," including those detained after the latest demonstrations.[116] Czechoslovaks opted for a non-violent approach, the so-called Velvet Revolution, to challenge the existing system.

The government coalition, the National Front, began coming apart, with junior partners talking to the opposition. In Bratislava, Dubcek delivered his first public address in two decades, and then joined with Havel on November 23 to speak to a crowd of 200,000 in Wenceslas Square. The next day, Jakes submitted his resignation, while massive rallies continued to take place.

On November 26, 1989, three-quarters of a million people congregated in Prague, followed the next day by a two-hour nationwide strike. The Federal Assembly discarded constitutional provisions guaranteeing the Communist Party's preeminent role, along with Marxism-Leninism as the official state ideology. New Communist Party leaders struggled to retain power, promising on December 3 to allow for fuller representation, genuine elections, protection of civil liberties, and removal of political pressures in places of employment. None of that sufficed, and on December 7, after 25,000 party members had resigned, Prime Minister Ladislav Adamec did as well. Three days later, the Communist government fell, with Husak resigning and a Government of National Understanding established. On December 28, the reconstituted Federal Assembly named Dubcek chairman, while the following day, it elected Havel president of the republic.

The new decade opened with grand expectations and considerable unity, even in provincial towns and rural areas where the appeal of the Velvet Revolution had initially been weaker than in major urban centers like Prague. In a New Year's address, Havel bemoaned the fact that Czechoslovakia was "not flourishing," with "enormous creative and spiritual potential" failing to be employed "meaningfully." The basic needs of the citizenry remained unmet, while "a state that calls itself a workers' state humiliates and exploits workers" and its "obsolete economy squanders our scarce energy resources," Havel continued. Additionally, its once proud educational level had plummeted, while the country was afflicted with "the most polluted environment in Europe." Still, Havel conveyed optimism, while affirming that "freedom and democracy must be based on participation and the acceptance of responsibility by everyone."[117]

Havel acknowledged that Czechoslovakia continued to be afflicted with the national question. He was bound, Havel indicated,

> to ensure that both nations approach the coming elections as truly self-governing, respecting each other's interests, national identity, religious traditions, and the fundamental symbols of nationhood. As a Czech in the office of president who swore his presidential oath to a famous Slovak and an intimate friend, I feel a particular responsibility to ensure that after the various bitter experiences the Slovaks have had, all the interests of the Slovak nation should be respected and that no offices of state be closed to its members.[118]

Havel's government thus clearly recognized that nationalism could become a disruptive political force, threatening the very stability of Czechoslovakia, along with the arbitrary borders it boasted. The new president also was aware that the expected adoption of free market economic practices would be unsettling to many, with the need to offer temporary subsidies as prices rose and to provide for the unemployed.

Changes occurred in rapid-fire succession. In February 1990, an accord was reached with the Soviet Union on the withdrawal of Red Army units from Czechoslovakia. (The last occupation forces did not depart until June 1991.) In April, the Federal Assembly passed the Law on State Enterprise, enabling the government to sell properties that had been nationalized in the late 1940s; the following year, a more expansive measure allowed for further privatization. The parliament also changed the name of the state from the Czechoslovak Socialist Republic to the Czech and Slovak Federative Republic. The following month, Soviet troops began departing from Czechoslovakia.

In June, Czechoslovakia experienced its first genuinely democratic elections since 1946, as 95 percent of eligible voters cast ballots. CF prevailed in the Czech Lands, taking a bare majority of the votes, while in Slovakia, VPN garnered a third of the ballots. Thus, the pair of civic movements pulled down 56 percent of the votes, while the Communist Party obtained the second highest total. On June 27, a new government was formed, drawn from the two civic movements, from the Christian Democratic Movement, and from individuals unaffiliated with specific political parties. The next week, the new parliament handed Havel a two-year term as president.

Havel possessed great stature as a champion of human rights and due to his own victimization at the hands of an authoritarian state. However, he had to contend with continuing economic difficulties, including a decline in the GNP (Gross National Product), a sharp reduction of exports to several Eastern European states, a balance of trade deficit, a soaring foreign debt, and inflation. Those economic ills only heightened already existing tensions between Czechs and Slovaks, who proved more resistant to economic reforms. By the end of the Communist era, the Slovak economy had managed to equal that of the Czech Lands, but it was saddled with large budgetary deficits and an over-reliance on heavy industry.

Nationalist demands mounted, leading to the transfer of power from the Federal Assembly to the two republics. The new constitution converted Czechoslovakia into a voluntary federation made up of those republics.

During the first half of 1991, Czechoslovakia continued to undergo considerable transformations. As the year opened, the Federal Assembly passed the Charter of Fundamental Rights and

Freedoms, affirming egalitarian and democratic principles, in addition to rule by law. The Charter outlawed capital punishment and forced labor or service; underscored "inviolability of the person and of privacy," along with sanctity of the home; guaranteed personal freedom, including freedom of movement, freedom of expression, and freedom of thought, conscience, and religion; and expressed the right to own property.[119]

Also, in the fashion of Western democratic states, the Charter underscored the right to petition government for redress of grievances, to assemble peacefully, to associate freely, and to participate in political affairs. One chapter highlighted the rights of national and ethnic minorities, including those involving the receipt of education in one's own language, the employment of that language in an official capacity, and the right to help resolve disputes centered around national and ethnic minorities.

Political changes occurred as well, some threatening the new nation's very makeup. Havel's efforts to hold the federation proved largely unavailing, and he suffered ridicule in the midst of a visit to Bratislava in early 1991. Even elements within VPN demanded guarantees regarding Slovakia's sovereignty, the possibility of which troubled the Hungarian minority. Increasingly, separatist demands became more heated, while a movement arose to rehabilitate the Slovak state and its right-wing leaders, including Jozef Tiso.

As developments threatened to escalate, Havel delivered a radio address on March 11, in which he referred to the "functioning, viable federation that still has some meaning." At the same time, he admitted that it would be more advisable "to have two independent republics" than "a nonfunctioning federation." Havel acknowledged that "the disintegration of the republic is an alternative that we have to consider seriously." Moreover, "If the Slovak nation prefers this solution, then it has a legitimate right to it."[120]

In April, CF split into the center-right Civic Democratic Party and the center-left Civic Movement, while various members joined the Social Democratic Party. VPN also splintered, with the Movement for Democratic Slovakia, which favored less accelerated economic reform, acquiring the largest backing among the electorate. Left-of-center forces possessed the support of approximately 60 percent of the populace in Slovakia.

By the summer, public frustration mounted in the face of continued economic difficulties. Following a failed coup by hard-line Communist forces in the Soviet Union, demands intensified for a purge of former supporters of the old regime and reformist communists, with even Dubcek targeted. Such a movement gathered more momentum in the Czech Lands than in Slovakia. Later in the year, negotiations crumbled as the Czech and Slovak governments considered a new federal constitution.

Clashes over federation continued through the first several months of 1992, leading up to general elections in early June. The Civic Democratic Party performed best in the Czech Lands, while the Movement for Democratic Slovakia did better still in Slovakia. Ironically enough, only the Communist Party competed throughout Czechoslovakia. Havel proceeded to run for reelection as president, but Slovak deputies refused to back him. Little support existed for separation, but Czech prime minister Vaclav Klaus and Slovak prime minister Vladimir Meciar now agreed to split the federation. On July 17 the Slovak National Council opted for "sovereignty."[121] The deeply disappointed Havel tendered his resignation, and the federal parliament struggled to find a candidate to replace him. At the beginning of October, the Federal Assembly voted to establish a Czech-Slovak union, but Klaus and Meciar worked to terminate the federation; on November 25, the Federal Assembly agreed to the separation. On January 1, 1993, the Czech Republic came into existence, while later in the month, Havel was elected president of the new state.

The Velvet Divorce, separating the Czech Lands and Slovakia, proceeded relatively seamlessly, with neither delivering territorial demands against the other, each containing few members of the other's leading ethnic groups, and both proving ready to divide assets in a 2:1 fashion befitting the disparate population

Alexander Dubcek speaks to a crowd of 500,000 Czechoslovakians on November 24, 1989, upon his return to the country after 20 years in exile. After the fall of the communist government during the Velvet Revolution, the reconstituted Federal Assembly named him chairman.

bases. Nevertheless, new arbitrary borders necessarily emerged, separating the two halves of the now former Czechoslovakia. The people of that disbanded state had hardly preferred separation, but as it occurred, the Czechs appeared to acquire "a new national identity" rather quickly.[122] The Czech Republic became a parliamentary republic, which experienced a tourist boom and possessed a strong industrial base. Little unemployment existed and prosperity appeared certain.

Indeed, within a decade, the Czech Republic possessed the highest standard of living in the region, although a reliance on market forces resulted in problems regarding housing, crime, and medical care. There also existed troublesome racism and discrimination directed against the Roma (Gypsies), among the 95 percent of the populace deemed ethnic Czechs. After decades of Communist rule, and with the two largest groups identifying themselves as Catholic or atheists, the lands making up the Czech Republic possessed generally progressive social policies regarding divorce, abortion, and sexual practices.

Relying on state-sponsored education, Czechs boasted a 98 percent literacy rate. In 1999, the Czech Republic joined the North Atlantic Treaty Organization, while five years later, it entered the European Union, an action favored by 77 percent of its residents. Appropriately enough, the nearly 80,000 square kilometers of the Czech Republic contained the historic regions of Slovakia and Bohemia, whose geographical borders framed the new state physically. Its democratic governance characterized the Czech Republic in other ways, differentiating it from the straitened nature of life under imperialism, Nazism, or Communism. Finally, the Czechs appeared free of the artificial boundaries that others had forced on them and on the Czech nation.

Seventh century B.C.	Iron-age settlements appear in Bohemia and Moravia.
Fifth century B.C.	Germanic forces move into Bohemia and Moravia.
Fifth century A.D.	Slavic tribes, including Czechs, move into Bohemia and Moravia.
Seventh century	Samo establishes mercantile empire, which falls apart after his death in 658.
Ninth century	Greater Moravian empire emerges.
924–935	Prince Vaclav reigns in Bohemia.
963	Bohemia becomes part of the Holy Roman Empire.
Tenth century	Premyslid dynasty solidifies.
Twelfth to Thirteenth centuries	German immigrants move into frontier territory, particularly adjacent to Bohemia.
Fourteenth century	Luxemburg dynasty begins in the early years of the century. Charles IV reigns, as Bohemia's ascendancy peaks. Charles founds Prague University (1348). A campaign to reform the Roman Catholic Church begins during his tenure.
Fifteenth century	This is the period of Jan Hus's greatest challenge to the Church. Deemed a heretic, he is burned at the stake in 1415.
1419–1436	The Hussite Wars break out.
1526	Czech nobles accept Ferdinand I of Habsburg as their ruler.
Sixteenth century	Protestant Reformation makes greater inroads among the general populace.
1618	Czech nobles revolt against the Habsburgs.
1618–1648	Thirty Years' War devastates Bohemia. Habsburg rule is reaffirmed.
1740–1780	Reign of Maria Theresa, who loses Silesia and Glatz, but retains control of Bohemia and Moravia.
1765–1790	Josef II serves as the Holy Roman Emperor. He enacts a series of reforms, including the discarding of serfdom, the issuance of the Tolerance Patent for religious freedom, and the expanding of educational opportunities.
1780s–1790s	Czech national revival begins. The French Revolution influences developments in the Czech Lands.

1800–1848 The industrial revolution intensifies, while further encouraging the emergence of Czech nationalism.

1848 Prague uprising occurs, but is thwarted, leading to reassertion of Habsburg dominance.

1848–1914 The Czech nationalist revival continues.

1868–1869 The Austrian-Hungarian Compromise establishes the Austro-Hungarian Monarchy, which is opposed by Czech nationalists.

1914–1918 World War I begins. Tomas Masaryk initiates campaign to obtain support for Czech independence. With Eduard Benes, Masaryk helps to found the

1348
Reign of Charles IV begins

1848
Prague revolution
is crushed

1526
Czech nobles
accept
Ferdinand I
of Habsburg
as their ruler

1938
Munich Agreement
results in the ceding
of Sudetenland
to Germany

1348

1939

1618
Thirty Years'
War begins

1939
Germany converts
Bohemia and
Moravia into a
protectorate

1419
Hussite Wars
break out

1918
Republic of
Czechoslovakia is
established

Czech External Committee, which reestablishes itself as the Czechoslovak National Council.

1918   Pittsburgh Agreement calls for a Czecho-Slovak state. Allied nations recognize the Czechoslovak National Council as the de facto Czechoslovak government. Tomas Masaryk becomes president of the republic of Czechoslovakia.

1929–1933   Height of the Great Depression, when unemployment and ethnic tensions soar. The pro-Nazi Sudeten-German Patriot Front emerges, soon to reappear as the Sudeten-German Party.

1945
Eduard Benes heads a coalition government

1968
Prague Spring unfolds, but Warsaw Pact troops invade Czechoslovakia

1989
Velvet Revolution overthrows the Communist government

1953
Joseph Stalin dies. The first visible signs of unrest in the Soviet bloc appear

1945

1993

1948
Communists conduct a coup to take over the Czechoslovak government

1956
Nikita Khrushchev condemns Stalinist terrors, shaking up Communist parties worldwide

1993
Czech Republic is established

1935 Czechoslovakia signs Treaties of Mutual Assistance with both the Soviet Union and France. Tomas Masaryk resigns as president of the republic, to be replaced by Benes.

1938 The Munich Agreement results in the ceding of the Sudetenland. Other territory is lost to Poland and Hungary.

1939 Germany annexes Bohemia and Moravia. Hitler establishes the Protectorate of Bohemia and Moravia. World War II begins. Hitler closes all Czech universities.

1940 Benes sets up a government-in-exile, recognized by Great Britain.

1941 Germans employ Czechs as forced laborers. German Nazi leader Reinhard Heydrich declares martial law and intensifies the reign of terror, in which thousands of Czechs are murdered or sent to concentration camps.

1942 Heydrich is assassinated, resulting in mass reprisals.

1945 Czechoslovakia is liberated. The Czechoslovak government, led by President Benes, returns to Prague. American and Soviet troops withdraw from Czechoslovakia.

1946 Nearly 2.2 million Germans are transferred from Czechoslovakia to Germany. In general elections, the Czechoslovak Communist Party receives more than 40 percent of the vote in the Czech Lands and over 30 percent of the vote total in Slovakia. Benes is reelected president, while Communist party leader Klement Gottwald is named prime minister.

1947 Czechoslovakia declines to participate in the Marshall Plan. Communists take control of Slovakia.

1948 Carrying out a coup, Czechoslovak Communist Party takes full control of the central government. Benes resigns as president, and is replaced by Gottwald.

1949–1952 Czechoslovakia joins COMECON. The Gottwald regime carries out purge trials. Collectivization of agriculture is accelerated.

1953–1955 Stalin and Gottwald die. Antonin Novotny heads the Czechoslovak Communist Party. The first visible signs of unrest occur in Eastern Europe. The last of the purge trials of the Communist era takes place. Czechoslovakia joins the Warsaw Pact.

1956 Soviet premier Nikita Khrushchev denounces Stalinist terrors at the twentieth party congress of the Soviet Communist Party. Poland and Hungary undergo reform, but Soviet troops crush the Hungarian Revolution.

1957–1963 The Czechoslovak Communist Party retains a hard-line stance. Economic difficulties mount, along with expressions of discontent by intellectuals.

1964 Leonid Brezhnev replaces Khrushchev as head of the Soviet Communist Party.

1964–1967 Foundation is laid for the Prague Spring. Limited attempts at market reform occur.

1968 Alexander Dubcek replaces Novotny as Czechoslovak Communist Party first secretary. The Prague Spring takes place, but produces a backlash among conservative Czechoslovak Communists and Warsaw Pact members. Warsaw Pact forces occupy Czechoslovakia. That nation's leaders are forced to sign the Moscow Protocol, condemning the Prague Spring.

1969 Gustav Husak replaces Dubcek as Czechoslovak Communist Party first secretary, as the process of normalization occurs.

1969–1972 Mass purges, along with arrests of leading intellectuals, are carried out.

1975 Husak becomes president of Czechoslovakia. The Helsinki Conference on Security and Cooperation in Europe highlights human rights concerns.

1977 The Charter 77 movement delivers its initial manifesto, which leads to the arrest of several signatories, including Vaclav Havel.

1984–1988 Mikhail Gorbachev becomes general secretary of the Soviet Communist Party. He initiates a program of reform based on *perestroika*, *glasnost*, and *demokratizatsiaa*.

1987 Milos Jakes replaces Husak as Czechoslovak Communist Party general secretary.

1988–1989 Protest against Communist rule intensifies. A police crackdown on demonstrators helps to spark the Velvet Revolution. The Civic Forum and Public Against Violence emerge. The Communist government collapses. Havel is elected president of the republic.

1990–1992 The name of the state is changed from "Czechoslovak Socialist Republic" to "Czech and Slovak Federative Republic." Dubcek is chosen chairman of the Federal Assembly, while Havel is reelected president. The Federal Assembly approves the Charter of Fundamental Rights and Freedoms. The Civic Forum and Public Against Violence both splinter. The final Soviet occupation troops depart. Czech prime minister Vaclav Klaus and Slovak prime minister Vladimir Meciar decide to divide Czechoslovakia, which the Federal Assembly agrees to.

1993 The Czech Republic is established; Havel is elected president.

Chapter 1

1. Quoted in Henri Nogueres, *Munich: "Peace for Our Time"* (New York: McGraw-Hill, 1965), p. 298.
2. Quoted in Keith Eubank, *Munich* (Norman, Oklahoma: University of Oklahoma Press, 1963), p. 227.
3. Quoted in Leon Blum, *Le Populaire*, September 20, 1938.
4. Quoted in Williamson Murray, *The Change in the European Balance of Power, 1938–1939: The Path to Ruin* (Princeton, New Jersey: Princeton University Press, 1984), p. 215.
5. Quoted in Tedford Taylor, *Munich: The Price of Peace* (Garden City, New York: Doubleday and Company, 1979), p. 57.
6. Quoted in Keith Eubank, "Munich," in *A History of the Czechoslovak Republic, 1918–1948*, eds. Victor S. Mamatey and Radomir Luza (Princeton, New Jersey: Princeton University Press, 1973), p. 240.
7. Quoted in Gerhard L. Weinberg, "Germany and Munich," in *Reappraising the Munich Pact: Continental Perspectives*, ed. Maya Latynski (Washington, D.C., and Baltimore: Woodrow Wilson Center Press and Johns Hopkins University Press, 1992), p. 9.
8. Quoted in Taylor, *Munich*, pp. 102, 296.
9. Ibid., pp. 300–301.
10. Quoted in J. W. Bruegel, *Czechoslovakia before Munich: The German Minority Problem and British Appeasement Policy* (Cambridge: Cambridge University Press, 1973), p. 187.
11. Quoted in Clement Leibovitz, *In Our Time: The Chamberlain-Hitler Collusion* (New York: Monthly Review Press, 1998), p. 117.
12. Quoted in Roy Douglas, *In the Year of Munich* (New York: St. Martin's Press, 1977), p. 27.
13. Ibid., p. 30.
14. Quoted in Murray, *The Change in the European Balance of Power*, p. 171.
15. Quoted in Nogueres, *Munich*, pp. 69–70.
16. Quoted in Murray, *Change in the European Balance of Power*, p. 184.
17. Quoted in Nogueres, *Munich*, p. 73.
18. Ibid., p. 84.
19. Quoted in Taylor, *Munich*, p. 698.
20. Quoted in Nogueres, *Munich*, p. 89.
21. Ibid., pp. 249–251.
22. Quoted in Nogueres, *Munich*, p. 115.
23. Quoted in Douglas, *In the Year of Munich*, p. 51.
24. Ibid., pp. 52, 54.
25. Quoted in Eubank, *Munich*, pp. 148, 150.
26. Quoted in Nogueres, *Munich*, p. 167.
27. Quoted in John R. Lampe, "Introduction," in Latynski, ed., *Reappraising the Munich Pact: Continental Perspectives*, p. 1.
28. Quoted in Nogueres, *Munich*, p. 180.
29. Quoted in Douglas, *In the Year of Munich*, pp. 62, 67.
30. Quoted in Eubank, *Munich*, p. 214.
31. Ibid., p. 229.

Chapter 2

32. Quoted in A.H. Hermann, *A History of the Czechs* (London: Allen Lane, 1975), p. 21.
33. Ibid., pp. 41, 43.
34. Ibid., p. 90.
35. Quoted in Derek Sayer, *The Coasts of Bohemia: A Czech History* (Princeton, New Jersey: Princeton University Press, 1998), pp. 59–60, 63, 64.
36. Ibid., p. 69.
37. Quoted in Stanley Z. Pech, *The Czech Revolution of 1848* (Chapel Hill, North Carolina: University of North Carolina Press, 1969), pp. 130, 133.

Chapter 3

38. Quoted in William V. Wallace, *Czechoslovakia* (Boulder, Colorado: Westview Press, 1976), p. 26.
39. Ibid., p. 34.
40. Ibid., p. 53.
41. Quoted in Victor S. Mamatey, "The Establishment of the Republic," in *A History of the Czechoslovak Republic, 1918–1948*, p. 4.
42. Quoted in Josef Kalvoda, *The Genesis of Czechoslovakia* (Boulder, Colorado: East European Monographs, 1986), pp. 3, 32.
43. Quoted in Mamatey, "The Establishment of the Republic," p. 11.

Chapter 4

44. Kalvoda, *The Genesis of Czechoslovakia*, p. 47.

45. Ibid., pp. 81, 83, 86.
46. Ibid., p. 88.
47. Ibid., p. 112.
48. Ibid., pp. 162–163.
49. Quoted in Mamatey, "The Establishment of the Republic," p. 16.
50. Ibid., p. 17.
51. Quoted in Hermann, *A History of the Czechs*, pp. 131–132.
52. Quoted in Wallace, *Czechoslovakia*, p. 112.
53. Quoted in Kalvoda, *The Genesis of Czechoslovakia*, p. 166.
54. Ibid., pp. 239, 241.
55. Ibid., p. 254.
56. Quoted in Mamatey, "The Establishment of the Republic," pp. 20–21.
57. Quoted in Kalvoda, *The Genesis of Czechoslovakia*, pp. 380, 391, 404.
58. Ibid., pp. 423–424.
59. Quoted in Stanislav J. Kirschbaum, *A History of Slovakia: The Struggle for Survival* (New York: St. Martin's Press, 1995), p. 149.
60. Quoted in Peter A. Toma and Dusan Kovac, *Slovakia: From Samo to Dzurinda* (Stanford: Stanford University Press, 2001), pp. 61, 64.

Chapter 5

61. Ibid., p. 68.
62. Quoted in Vaclav L. Benes, "Czechoslovak Democracy and Its Problems, 1918–1920," in *A History of the Czechoslovak Republic, 1918–1948*, pp. 45, 96.
63. Quoted in John O. Crane and Sylvia Crane, *Czechoslovakia: Anvil of the Cold War* (New York: Praeger, 1991).
64. Quoted in Wallace, *Czechoslovakia*, p. 190.
65. Quoted in Victor S. Mamatey, "The Development of Czechoslovak Democracy, 1920–1938," in *A History of the Czechoslovak Republic, 1918–1938*, p. 148.
66. Quoted in Rick Fawn, *The Czech Republic: A Nation of Velvet* (Amsterdam: Harwood Academic Publishers, 2000), pp. 7–8.
67. Quoted in Hermann, *A History of the Czechs*, p. 267.

Chapter 6

68. Quoted in Theodor Prochazka, "The Second Republic, 1938–1939," in *A History of the Czechoslovak Republic, 1918–1948*, pp. 256–257.
69. Ibid., pp. 267–268.
70. Quoted in Crane and Crane, *Czechoslovakia*, p. 175.
71. Ibid., pp. 185, 187.
72. Quoted in Fawn, *The Czech Republic*, p. 9.
73. Quoted in Gotthold Rhode, "The Protectorate of Bohemia and Moravia, 1939–1945," in *A History of the Czechoslovak Republic, 1918–1948*, p. 308.
74. Quoted in Crane and Crane, *Czechoslovakia*, p. 200.
75. Quoted in Edward Taborsky, "Politics in Exile, 1939–1945," in *A History of the Czechoslovak Republic, 1918–1948*, p. 334.
76. Quoted in Crane and Crane, *Czechoslovakia*, pp. 213–214.
77. Ibid., p. 242.
78. Quoted in Radomir Luza, "Czechoslovakia between Democracy and Communism, 1945–1948," in *A History of the Czechoslovak Republic, 1918–1948*, p. 405.

Chapter 7

79. Quoted in Carol Skalnik Leff, *The Czech and Slovak Republics: Nation Versus State* (Boulder, Colorado: Westview Press, 1997), p. 49.
80. Quoted in Wallace, *Czechoslovakia*, p. 275.
81. Leff, *The Czech and Slovak Republics*, p. 48.
82. Quoted in Wallace, *Czechoslovakia*, p. 291.
83. Ibid., p. 294.
84. Quoted in Fawn, *The Czech Republic*, p. 18.
85. Quoted in Kenneth N. Skoug Jr., *Czechoslovak's Lost Fight for Freedom, 1967–1969: An American Embassy Perspective.* (Westport, Connecticut: Praeger, 1999), pp. 6–7.
86. Quoted in in Jeremi Suri, *Power and Protest: Global Revolution and the Rise of Détente* (Cambridge, Massachusetts: Harvard University Press, 2003), p. 195.

Chapter 8

87. Quoted in Skoug, *Czechoslovak's Lost Fight for Freedom*, p. 28.
88. Quoted in Suri, *Power and Protest*, pp. 194–195.
89. Quoted in Skoug, *Czechoslovak's Lost Fight for Freedom*, p. 41.
90. Ibid., p. 47.
91. Ibid., p. 46.
92. Quoted in Suri, *Power and Protest*, p. 198.
93. Quoted in Skoug, *Czechoslovak's Lost Fight for Freedom*, p. 64.
94. Ibid., p. 68.
95. Quoted in Mark Kramer, "The Czechoslovak Crisis and the Brezhnev Doctrine," in *1968: The World Transformed*, ed. Carole Fink, Philipp Gassert, and Detlef Junker (Washington, D.C.: Cambridge University Press, 1999), p. 123.
96. Quoted in Suri, *Power and Protest*, p. 198.
97. Quoted in Skoug, *Czechoslovakia's Lost Fight for Freedom*, pp. 74–75.
98. Ibid., p. 79.
99. Ibid., p. 90.
100. Quoted in Suri, *Power and Protest*, p. 199.
101. Quoted in Kramer, "The Czechoslovak Crisis and the Brezhnev Doctrine," pp. 127–128.
102. Ibid., pp. 132–134.
103. Quoted in Leff, *The Czech and Slovak Republics*, p. 57.
104. Quoted in Skoug, *Czechoslovakia's Lost Fight for Freedom*, p. 114.
105. Quoted in Ludvik Vaculik, "Two Thousand Words," June 27, 1968.
106. Quoted in Skoug, *Czechoslovakia's Lost Fight for Freedom*, pp. 117–118.
107. Ibid., pp. 173–174.
108. Quoted in Vladimir V. Kusin, *From Dubcek to Charter 77: A Study of 'Normalization' in Czechoslovakia, 1968–1978.* (New York: St. Martin's Press, 1978), pp. 149, 151.
109. Ibid., p. 156.

Chapter 9

110. The Declaration of Charter 77, January 1, 1977.
111. Quoted in Jan Kavan, "From the Prague Spring to a Long Winter," in the *Prague Spring: A Mixed Legacy*, ed. Jiri Pehe (Landham, Maryland: Freedom House, 1988), p. 122.
112. Ibid., pp. 119, 123.
113. Ibid., p. 123.
114. Quoted in Bernard Wheaton and Zdenek Kavan, *The Velvet Revolution: Czechoslovakia, 1988–1991* (Boulder, Colorado: Westview Press, 1992), pp. 18, 26.
115. Ibid., p. 35.
116. Quoted in "Proclamation of the Founding of Citizens Forum," November 19, 1989.

Chapter 10

117. Quoted in Wheaton and Kavan, *The Velvet Revolution*, p. 129.
118. Ibid., p. 137.
119. Quoted in "Charter of Fundamental Rights and Freedoms," January 9, 1991.
120. Quoted in Wheaton and Kavan, *The Velvet Revolution*, p. 171.
121. Quoted in Fawn, *The Czech Republic*, p. 34.
122. Ibid., p. 35.

Benes, Vaclav L. "Czechoslovak Democracy and Its Problems, 1918–1920," in *The History of the Czechoslovak Republic, 1918–1948*, eds. Victor S. Mamatey and Radomir Luza. Princeton: Princeton University Press, 1973.

Bruegel, J.W. *Czechoslovakia Before Munich: The German Minority Problem and British Appeasement Policy*. Cambridge: Cambridge University Press, 1973.

Crane, John O., and Sylvia Crane. *Czechoslovakia: Anvil of the Cold War*. New York: Praeger, 1991.

Douglas, Roy. *In the Year of Munich*. New York: St. Martin's Press, 1977.

Eubank, Keith. "Munich," in *The History of the Czechoslovak Republic, 1918–1948*, eds.

Victor S. Mamatey and Radomir Luza, eds. *The History of the Czechoslovak Republic, 1918–1948*. Princeton: Princeton University Press, 1973.

———. *Munich*. Norman: University of Oklahoma Press, 1963.

Fawn, Rick. *The Czech Republic: A Nation of Velvet*. Amsterdam: Harwood Academic Publishers, 2000.

Fink, Carole, Philipp Gassert, and Detlef Junker, eds. *1968: The World Transformed*. Cambridge: Cambridge University Press, 1999.

Hermann, A.H. *A History of the Czechs*. London: Allen Lane, 1975.

Kalvoda, Josef. *The Genesis of Czechoslovakia*. New York: Columbia University Press, 1986.

Kirschbaum, Stanislav J. *A History of Slovakia: The Struggle for Survival*. New York: St. Martin's Press, 1995.

Kramer, Mark. "The Czechoslovak Crisis and the Brezhnev Doctrine," in *1968: The World Transformed*. eds. Fink, Carole, Philipp Gassert, and Detlef Junker. Cambridge: Cambridge University Press, 1999.

Kusin, Vladimir. *From Dubcek to Charter 77: A Study of "Normalization" in Czechoslovakia, 1968–1978*. New York: St. Martin's Press, 1978.

Lampe, John. "Introduction," in *Reappraising the Munich Pact: Continental Perspectives*, ed. Latynski, Maya. Washington, D. C. and Baltimore: Woodrow Wilson Center Press and John Hopkins Press, 1992.

Latynski, Maya, ed. *Reappraising the Munich Pact: Continental Perspectives*. Washington, D. C. and Baltimore: Woodrow Wilson Center Press and John Hopkins Press, 1992.

Leff, Carol Skalnik. *The Czech and Slovak Republics: Nation Versus State*. Boulder, Colorado: Westview Press, 1997.

Leibovitz, Clement, and Alvin Finkel. *In Our Time: The Chamberlain-Hitler Collusion*. New York: Monthly Review Press, 1998.

Mamatey, Victor S. "The Development of Czechoslovak Democracy, 1920–1938," in *The History of the Czechoslovak Republic, 1918–1948*, eds. Mamatey, Victor S., and Radomir Luza. Princeton: Princeton University Press, 1973.

———. "The Establishment of the Republic," in *The History of the Czechoslovak Republic, 1918–1948*, eds. Mamatey, Victor S,. and Radomir Luza. Princeton: Princeton University Press, 1973.

Mamatey, Victor S., and Radomir Luza, eds. *The History of the Czechoslovak Republic*, Princeton: Princeton University Press, 1973.

Murray, Williamson. *The Change in the European Balance of Power, 1938–1939: The Path to Ruin*. Princeton: Princeton University Press, 1984.

Nogueres, Henri. *Munich: "Peace for Our Time."* New York: McGraw-Hill, 1965.

Pech, Stanley Z. *The Czech Revolution of 1848*. Chapel Hill: University of North Carolina Press, 1969.

Pehe, Jiri, ed. *The Prague Spring: A Mixed Legacy*. New York: Freedom House, 1988.

Prochazka, Theodor. "The Second Republic, 1938–1939," in *The History of the Czechoslovak Republic, 1918–1948,* eds. Mamatey, Victor S., and Radomir Luza. Princeton: Princeton University Press, 1973.

Rhode, Gotthold. "The Protectorate of Bohemia and Moravia, 1939–1945," in *The History of the Czechoslovak Republic, 1918–1948,* eds. Mamatey, Victor S., and Radomir Luza. Princeton: Princeton University Press, 1973.

Sayer, Derek. *The Coasts of Bohemia: A Czech History.* Princeton: Princeton University Press, 1998.

Skoug, Kenneth N. Jr. *Czechoslovakia's Lost Fight for Freedom, 1967–1969: An American Embassy Perspective.* Westport, Connecticut: Praeger, 1999.

Taylor, Telford. *Munich: The Price for Peace.* New York: Doubleday, 1979.

Suri, Jeremi. *Power and Protest: Global Revolution and the Rise of Détente.* Cambridge, Massachusetts: Harvard University Press, 2003.

Toma, Peter A., and Dusan Kovac. *Slovakia: From Samo to Dzurinda.* Stanford: Hoover Institution Press, 2001.

Wallace, William V. *Czechoslovakia.* Boulder, Colorado: Westview Press, 1976.

Weinberg, Gerhard L. "Germany and Munich," in *Reappraising the Munich Pact: Continental Perspectives,* ed. Latynski, Maya. Washington, D.C. and Baltimore: Woodrow Wilson Center Press and John Hopkins Press, 1992.

Wheaton, Bernard, and Zdenek Kavan. *The Velvet Revolution: Czechoslovakia, 1988–1991.* Boulder, Colorado: Westview Press, 1992.

Bartos, F.M. *The Hussite Revolution, 1424–1437.* Boulder, Colorado: East European Monographs, 1986.

Bedford, Neal, Jane Rawson, and Matt Warren. *Czech & Slovak Republics.* Malaysia: Lonely Planet, 2004.

Bradley, J.F.N. *Czechoslovakia: A Short History.* Edinburgh: University Press, 1971.

Garton Ash, Timothy. *We the People: The Revolutions of 1989.* London: Granta, 1990.

Havel, Vaclav. *Living in Truth,* ed. Jan Vladislav. London: Faber & Faber, 1986.

Hitchcock, William I. *The Struggle for Europe: The Turbulent History of a Divided Continent, 1945–2002.* New York: Doubleday, 2003.

Hochman, Jiri. *Historical Dictionary of the Czech State.* Lanham, Maryland: Scarecrow Press, 1998.

Holy, Ladislav, *The Little Czech and the Great Czech Nation: National Identity and the Post-Communist Social Transformation.* Cambridge: Cambridge University Press, 1996.

Kaplan, Karel. *The Short March: The Communist Takeover of Power in Czechoslovakia, 1945–1948.* Oxford: Holdan Books, 1985.

Korbel, Josef. *Twentieth-Century Czechoslovakia: The Meaning of Its History.* New York: Columbia University Press, 1977.

Krejci, Josef, and Pavel Machonin. *Czechoslovakia, 1918–92: A Laboratory for Social Change.* London: Macmillan, 1996.

Kurlansky, Mark. *1968: The Year that Rocked the World.* New York: Ballantine Books, 2004.

Leff, Carol Skalnik. *National Conflict in Czechoslovakia: The Making and Remaking of a State, 1918–1987.* Princeton: Princeton University Press, 1988.

Macartney, C.A. *The Habsburg Empire, 1790–1918.* London: Lawrence and Nicolson, 1969.

Myant, Martin. *Socialism and Democracy in Czechoslovakia, 1945–1948.* Cambridge: Cambridge University Press, 1981.

Prochazka, Theodore Sr. *The Second Republic: The Disintegration of Post-Munich Czechoslovakia (October 1938–October 1939).* Boulder, Colorado: East European Monographs, 1981.

Renner, Hans. *A History of Czechoslovakia Since 1945.* London: Routledge, 1989.

Shawcross, William. *Dubcek: Dubcek and Czechoslovakia, 1918–1990.* London: Hogarth Press, 1990.

Skilling, H. Gordon. *Czechoslovakia's Interrupted Revolution.* Princeton: Princeton University Press, 1976.

Williams, Kieran. *The Prague Spring and Its Aftermath.* Cambridge: Cambridge University Press, 1997.

Zeman, Zdenek. *The Masaryks: The Making of Czechoslovakia.* London: Taurus, 1990.

page:

9: Associated Press, OFFICE OF WAR INFORMATION
10: Associated Press
16: © Getty Images
19: © Getty Images
31: Library of Congress, LC-USZ62-100456
41: © Getty Images
53: © Bettmann/CORBIS

68: Library of Congress, LC-USZ62-105584
75: Associated Press
82: © Getty Images
89: © Time Life Pictures/Getty Images
96: Associated Press, CTK
105: Associated Press, AP
115: © Peter Turnley/CORBIS
121: © Peter Turnley/CORBIS

Frontis: Courtesy The United Nations Cartographic Section, Map No. 3849 Rev. 4, August 2004

Robert C. Cottrell, Professor of History and American Studies at California State University, Chico, is the author of many books, including *Izzy: A Biography of I.F. Stone, Roger Nash Baldwin and the American Civil Liberties Union, The Best Pitcher in Baseball: The Life of Rube Foster, Negro League Giant,* and *Uncertain Order: The World in the Twentieth Century.* Named the Outstanding Professor at CSUC in 1998, Professor Cottrell received the 2000 Wang Family Excellence Award for Social & Behavioral Sciences & Public Services, a system-wide honor for the 23 campuses that make up the California State University.

George J. Mitchell served as chairman of the peace negotiations in Northern Ireland during the 1990s. Under his leadership, an historic accord, ending decades of conflict, was agreed to by the governments of Ireland and the United Kingdom and the political parties in Northern Ireland. In May 1998, the agreement was overwhelmingly endorsed by a referendum of the voters of Ireland, North and South. Senator Mitchell's leadership earned him worldwide praise and a Nobel Peace Prize nomination. He accepted his appointment to the U.S. Senate in 1980. After leaving the Senate, Senator Mitchell joined the Washington, D.C. law firm of Piper Rudnick, where he now practices law. Senator Mitchell's life and career have embodied a deep commitment to public service and he continues to be active in worldwide peace and disarmament efforts.

James I. Matray is professor of history and chair at California State University, Chico. He has published more than forty articles and book chapters on U.S.-Korean relations during and after World War II. Author of *The Reluctant Crusade: American Foreign Policy in Korea, 1941–1950* and *Japan's Emergence as a Global Power,* his most recent publication is *East Asia and the United States: An Encyclopedia of Relations Since 1784.* Matray also is international columnist for the *Donga Ilbo* in South Korea.

144